Advance Praise for Kristin Beck, Anne Speckhard and
<u>Warrior Princess</u>:

"Speckhard and Beck have teamed up to give us one of the smartest and most important books of the year. <u>Warrior Princess</u> is the story of Kristin Beck, formerly Chris, a decorated Navy SEAL and American patriot who faced a lifelong struggle to come to terms with her gender identity.

The book could stand alone as an account of Beck's distinguished career in the military, but <u>Warrior Princess</u> has a bolder message to send to its readers: transgender people are people... and some of them are even our national heroes.

Beck is a natural protagonist...strong, hardworking, and deeply patriotic. Every reader can relate to her, whether it's her coming of age story, her decision to join the elite Navy SEALs, or even her coming to terms with her gender identity. And where Kristin's experiences differ from the readers, Speckhard subtly exercises her understanding of psychology and sociology to bridge the gap.

Whether a pacifist or a hawk, advocate or opponent of LGBT equality, <u>Warrior Princess</u> is a raw, honest, and surprisingly relatable read."—*Out-Serve Magazine*

"<u>Warrior Princess</u> is a profile of courage, both physical and personal. It shatters one's perceptions of what courage is and how it is shown. Courage isn't just about physical bravery, it is also about personal bravery. Being transgender requires a type of bravery very few could show, even by those who have been in combat. Dr. Anne Speckhard does a marvelous job of taking us on a journey about being transgender in the military. <u>Warrior Princess</u> should be required reading by anyone supporting and taking care of our troops, whether they support transgender issues or not."—*Colonel Carl A. Castro (U.S. Army, retired)*

"Kristin Beck is a woman of extraordinary courage. Her story is an inspiration to all and a call to arms for those who wish to live authentically. Her bravery as a SEAL rivals the bravery she exhibits in crossing the seemingly inviolable gender boundary. Ms. Beck is a hero who has sacrificed for her country and shed light on this most misunderstood area of human behavior."—*Randi Ettner, Ph.D., author of Gender Loving Care, Confessions of a Gender Defender; editor, of Principles of Transgender Medicine and Surgery*

"As a Vietnam vet who saw more combat in the sixties than any man should see in a lifetime, I related to Kristin's book more than anything I have read in a long time. I have been a cross-dresser and this gives me courage. I am now out in the two worlds and hope to find my own peace. I believe this book could help many people come "out" in any way and live the life they wish."—*George Massarella, 173rd Airborne Brigade, Central Highlands Vietnam; 4th Infantry Division, I Corps, Vietnam*

"Military service in combat is so deeply meaningful to those who experience it that you can feel the undercurrent of emotion in the stories they tell. Gender transition is like that, too; difficult to explain to those who haven't been there, but deeply meaningful to those who have. This story trembles with the intensity of both experiences, and touches the best in humanity in both worlds, without ignoring the brutality that we must also acknowledge exists. A testament to bravery, Warrior Princess reaches for the best in all of us."—*Jamison Green, Ph.D., author of Becoming a Visible Man*

"Though Chris had a military career beyond what most experience, Kristin's journey will be all too familiar to the transgender people currently serving. This is a book about courage, and one that should challenge our notions of what heroism looks like."—*Indra Lusero, J.D. Director, Transgender Military Initiative, Palm Center*

"There's no need for the military to be a one-size-fits-all world. This story will widen your perspective about the meaning of gender and how much it matters—or doesn't—for successful military service. This inspiring account is also written for anyone working with veterans and their transition to civilian life, no matter what the issues might be."—*Diane H. Mazur, University of Florida law professor, former Air Force officer, and author of A More Perfect Military: How the Constitution Can Make Our Military Stronger (Oxford University Press)*

"This momentous book shares vividly the real life experiences of a veteran SEAL who goes on to transition as a civilian. The raw adrenaline packed events explicitly describe growing up, marriage, combat and leave and are experienced through anecdotes to the audience. The dramatic combat action and the shared emotional responses to both the war and the gender dysphoria are conviction of the traumas of both combat and transition. The book will be an inspiration to individuals struggling with gender dysphoria and seeking to find a way forwards. It will be a useful resource to share with important family members and friends to read in advance or alongside sharing plans of the change ahead for an individual."—*Professor Kevan Wylie, MD FRCP FRCPsych FRCOG; Director, World Professional Association for Transgender Health; President, World Association for Sexual Health*

"As Kristin Beck is showing us, gender expectations are for the birds. You can be anything in this life regardless of gender identity and, best of all, be true to yourself because of it."—*Thomas Beatie, author of Labor of Love: The Story of One Man's Extraordinary Pregnancy*

"To show that even a strong and patriotic Navy SEAL can be a transgender person totally blows away any stereotype of who trans people really are."—*Monica Helms, Founder and President of the Transgender American Veterans Association and author of Tales from a Two-Gendered Mind*

"Kristin Beck is to be commended for her courage under fire in the service of this great country and for her determination to share her story in spite of the negative consequences that most transgender people face when they come out. <u>Warrior Princess</u> is an action-packed book that demonstrates the "flight into hypermasculinity" I have observed in so many Veterans and active duty service members over the past thirty years of providing transgender health care in federal settings. There are thousands of transgender Veterans who can resonate with Kristin's story and benefit from the honesty embodied in this book. I highly recommend this exciting story as a modern day, amped up, sequel to memoirs from transgender Veterans such as Christine Jorgenson who have helped pave the path to acceptance over many years of struggle."—*George R. Brown, MD, DFAPA Professor of Psychiatry, East Tennessee State University, Member - Board of Directors World Professional Association for Transgender Health, former active duty military psychiatrist*

WARRIOR PRINCESS

A U.S. NAVY SEAL'S JOURNEY TO COMING OUT TRANSGENDER

Kristin Beck, U.S. Navy SEAL (Ret.)
&
Anne Speckhard, Ph.D.

First published 2013
by Advances Press
McLean, VA

Book Design by Nikki Hensley (www.hensleygraphics.com)
Editing by Jayne Pillemer
Cover Design by Kristin Beck & Jessica Speckhard
Photos courtesy of Kristen Beck
Professional photographs found in Third Life section by Christy Borjes
(http://www.borjesphotography.com)

Every effort has been made to contact and acknowledge copyright own-
ers, but the author and publisher would be pleased to have any errors or
omissions brought to their attention so that corrections may be published
at a later printing.

Library of Congress Control Number: 2013936593

ISBN 978-1-935866-42-8 –Warrior Princess—Hardcover
ISBN 978-1-935866-43-5 –Warrior Princess—Paperback
ISBN 978-1-935866-44-2 –Warrior Princess—E-Pub

DEDICATION

This book is dedicated to my family who supported me through the years, the good and the bad, the joy and the anguish. Thank you.

To my SEAL brothers for the twenty years of Teams and Shit and the many missions we did during the wars. I am still the same person with the same experience and the same spirit.

To the underdogs, the activists, the down trodden who catch up and sometimes even surpass and triumph. Keep up the fight! And keep the faith; you have to be in the fight to make any changes.

Kristin Beck

TABLE OF CONTENTS

FOREWORD

I first met Chris Beck in the summer of 2001 when we were both assigned to the SEAL Staff Headquarters in Coronado California. Chris was nearing the end of his tour and rotating back into an operational SEAL team. He had just developed a unique computer-based tool for the SEAL's operational planning. I had seen similar products before in NASA's space program, built by teams of engineers at large aerospace companies. Chris had done this himself, without requirements or any top-level support. The software became a breakthrough capability that was quickly adopted in the SEAL teams. I knew then that Chris had some exceptional "MacGyver" qualities. Chris would often show up at a local bar on a custom motorcycle he built in his spare time. When he returned to the SEAL teams, he modified a desert patrol vehicle for special surveillance and fire support roles. Though the SEAL community prides itself in being able to think "out of the box", conformity is often the reality. Chris probably didn't think there was a "box".

Ten years later, I worked with Chris again at the Special Operations Command Headquarters in Florida. Chris was finishing up his active duty SEAL career and joined me in the "Science and Technology" Directorate. Chris helped to create portable, "make anything" fabrication shops on the battlefield, close to the operators. He planned the layout of the fab facilities, built the training curriculum, and led the combat deployments of the boxes and the technical teams to Afghanistan. Today these fab shops are a key part of Special Ops forces' innovation network. The project has created thousands of new capabilities—and saved lives. Chris is one of the most intuitive and creative thinkers I have ever met.

Chris and I shared a common background—getting through Basic Underwater Demolition SEAL training (BUD/S). It's the toughest training in the military—any military. The training requires perseverance and commitment. Often, well more than half of the "trainees" quit—by ringing a bell in the training area. I thought "ringing out' sometimes took more courage than to stay in the ranks where you "fit in". Ringing out was an admission—that you were an anomaly, different. Chris is now Kristen. I thought about how I would relate to the change. I remembered an event I saw in my NASA days, when Space Shuttle Atlantis docked to the Russian space station Mir, twenty years ago. The two space vehicles were flying amid many doubts that two Cold War rivals could work together in a hostile environment—where crews had to get along to survive. One of the cosmonauts remarked on the radio as the two space vehicles linked up:

"We are now one. . . . We are all human."

William "Shep" Shepherd
Virginia, Beach VA
May 18, 2013

PRESS RELEASE

February 9, 2013

Chris Beck—U.S. Navy Senior Chief (retired); SEAL Team operator and decorated war hero—has recently announced his long-standing gender identity as a female. Chris Beck proudly served this country as a U.S. Navy SEAL for over twenty years, serving on three different SEAL teams. Chris was deployed thirteen times, serving in Bosnia, Afghanistan and Iraq and earned both the Bronze Star with "V," the Purple Heart, and various other personal awards for her leadership and innovative spirit. Following retirement from military service in 2011, Chris has since continued service to our country by working for the Secretary of Defense in the Rapid Reaction Technology Office.

While in active duty status, Chris respectfully remained silent regarding her gender identity—following the U.S. military's "don't ask/don't tell" policy current during her service—but since retirement has decided to announce her decision to live openly and as authentically as possible. As a disabled wounded warrior, Chris is receiving professional support from the Veterans Administration and the Special Operations Care Coalition at MacDill Air force Base to meet the challenges of this period of her life.

In an attempt to reach out to others who may face similar challenges, while keeping the sincerest respect to "The Brotherhood", Chris is documenting her life in a non-fiction book that will be released from Advances Press soon. It is her deepest desire that after having fought for this country's freedoms, she too will be afforded the freedom to live in a manner consistent with her life-long gender awareness as a female.

PREFACE

This is *a* story. It's Kristin Beck's story as told to Anne Speckhard—a research psychologist and friend. It's not *the* story, as it's impossible to ever know or tell one's whole story. So much of what happens in our childhood and shaped our lives is only known by the one who lived it—if remembered at all—in fragments that are distorted through the multiple lenses of long-term memory and a child's perspective. Kristin's story is continuing on even after this book; who knows where it will lead. She has an eye on politics or the position of Director of the Science & Technology Programs at the Pentagon.

So much of what has shaped us on an unconscious and unknown level, what's encoded in our genes and expresses itself because of our experiences—or in spite of them—and what is hidden in our souls is mostly not known and never discovered by most of us. Kristin did her best to tell his story to Anne, and Anne did her best to convey it as fairly as possible without the benefits of school and medical records from that time period or the viewpoints of Kristin's family members, whose names have been changed here to protect their privacy.

It should be noted to the reader that throughout this book we have opted to refer to Kristin in the here and now and recent past as she, and to Chris living as a boy, young man and as a U.S. Navy SEAL as he. Likewise when Kris is looking back in the here and now commenting on her former life as a Navy SEAL, a young man, or a child we have referred to Kris recalling as she, a body and self that was and is still known as he. We hope this isn't confusing.

Kristin recalls always feeling that she was a female—or at least she wanted to be female—and felt as a young child and throughout her life—up till now—that she was trapped in a male body and defined as a male. There are theories and posits on all sides about why and how this happens. One thing is certain, people are all different and we are all on the same planet; at the end we all arrive at the same place.

Born Chris Beck, Kris spent the first part of her adult life as a natural male working as a U.S. Navy SEAL. Chris suppressed the angst of feeling that he was a female in a male's body during that time (twenty years of service to our country) as he earned his way into the toughest male profession that exists and served on thirteen deployments around the world.

Chris describes his despair throughout this book and his desire to die honorably by serving our country and fighting terrorism— to keep us safe and so that he wouldn't have to wrestle anymore with the emotional pain that stemmed from the lack of congruency between his gender identity and body. After multiple combat deployments—more than many SEALs ever encounter, Chris returned alive to fight this deeper battle in his soul and grappled with the moral and social decisions of living in secret or to transition into her true self.

No one knows exactly how gender identity disorders occur. We do know that in the U.S. alone seven hundred thousand people identify themselves as transgender—and that's only the ones brave enough to admit it. And we know that gender identity, while certainly a social construct on many levels, is in part formed by our families and our experiences in childhood. Sexuality and even identity also has a genetic component that we still don't understand. The complex idea of gender may never be fully understood, but with acceptance and compassion on all parts we may come to peace with the fact that identifying oneself by gender is a fundamental part of the "human experience" and likely always will be.

Chris told Anne about his early life, what he saw as the formative influences in his childhood; and she, as a research psychologist, teased out more information and together they pieced it together into this story. In the interest of protecting classified information or sensitive tactical details of the SEALS, a few of the stories are composites of actual events in which some events are fictionalized but the essential truth remains. Suffice it to say, the true story is that Chris served in seven combat deployments of thirteen total deployments and earned many medals including the Purple Heart and the Bronze Star with "V" for valor.

As much as possible Anne and Chris both tried to honor Chris's family. His parents did their best. All parents bring their own familial and personal history to bear in how they respond to the task of parenting. And in the sixties and seventies Dr. Spock had a great deal of influence to boot. It's almost impossible to raise and shape a child while dealing with all of life's stressors and challenges without failing in some ways—without causing some damage—and leaving behind some scars on the soul. In this regard, Chris's parents are no different.

Chris's family struggles with accepting the concept of him as a female caught in a male's body, yet they were a large part of the forces that created that situation. And of course there were other forces that no one fully understands. Chris hopes that eventually his family will come to some peace about it and find love and acceptance, as directed by the best virtues of a Christian life despite their moral reservations and discomfort. He also hopes they can find peace and accept his choice to find authenticity in his life by choosing to make his body match his inner self rather than struggling further to suppress or attempt to change that inner self.

Chris is a father to two boys and he's been a husband twice. He loves his children, although he's ashamed that in serving his country non-stop for twenty years as a Navy SEAL and in his wish to avoid dealing with his own issues, he missed most of his sons' lives. He'd like to make that up to his two sons and hopes they can accept his painful choices. He loves his first wife. She's been a great mother—loyal and true to her task of taking care of her husband and raising their sons, which she did mostly alone without Chris's presence. He is eternally grateful to her for all she's done for their sons and so sorry he could not be the husband she—and he—both wished he could have been. Chris appreciates his second wife too; they both understood much faster that it was a mistake to try to force a square peg into a round hole. Chris could not be the man she needed, and he's sorry for that too.

Chris also has thousands of other brothers in the Teams—the Navy SEALs—and he's proud of his "Frogman" family. He knows what it took to gain entry to "The Brotherhood" and he would never dishonor that fraternity. He will never forget his time serving alongside warriors who he still feels were his better—men who died when he survived. He'd have given his life to save any of them. He's sorry if he's causing any discomfort or embarrassment to "The Brother-hood". He loves the guys he served with and dreams that someday after all the hormones and the transitioning to a female body, that as Kristin she will return to train the women who will likely—soon enough and inevitably—be trying out to become SEALs alongside the men.

It took great courage in the last years to decide to live authenti-cally and become Kristin: the woman who so needed to live. It also took great courage to share what's in this book—to put a very personal struggle out to the public, hopefully to help others come to a place of love and acceptance. It's so easy to judge and condemn, especially without at least trying to understand. Maybe this book can explain how Senior Chief Chris Beck, U.S. Navy SEAL, served his country honorably and beyond what most would only dream, as a man—and later became a woman and activist for compassion and peace.

That is certainly my hope as her friend.

Anne Speckhard, Ph.D. —Washington, D.C.

~

After I retired from the SEALs I started a journey into unknown territory for myself. I found a large number of people with similar issues and found that there is a huge misconception in the American public and even the medical community on gender. I am mournful of the great loss due to gender identity in America; the suicide rate amongst Trans* is nearly 50% compared to societies norm of around 2%. THIS IS THE PRIMARY REASON FOR THIS BOOK. I reach out to all of the younger generation and encourage you to live your life fully and to treat each other with compassion, be good to each other especially in your own backyard (whether it be high school and your community). There is a huge world out there and many adventures await you. Live and be happy.

In my way of thinking everyone has at least two lives they could live. The first life everyone is born into, and you have zero choice in that first life. In my case, my first life is defined by the 1960s, American, Swedish/Norwegian decent, reddish-brown hair, male, 5'10", Christian, lower middle class on a farm in the middle of nowhere.

The second life is when you get a job or do something of your choosing as an adult. My second life was gained through my childhood, my education, family, friends, the military and the U.S. Navy SEALs. I did my best in my first two lives and I lived them fully with no regrets and no remorse. I cherish the time I had and would not change a thing.

I see this as a new life for myself—as a third chance to live. Most people never attempt a third life, even if they need or want it. My third life will be Kristin—the journey that will make me whole! Anyone can make this leap into any unknown, difficult terrain if they have the courage. This change does not have to be as drastic as mine; maybe you are a lawyer and you always needed to be a grade schoolteacher or an inventor. I do not believe a soul has a gender, but my new path is making my soul complete and happy. I hope my journey sheds some light on the human experience and most importantly helps heal the "socio-religious dogma" of a purely binary gender.

Kristin Beck, U.S. Navy SEAL (Ret.)

PROLOGUE

Chris in gear in Afghanistan.

Hot Zone

The rotors beat the air as the helicopter made its way through Afghanistan's night sky. Gazing around him, Senior Chief Beck saw the green glow of the night vision goggles fitted over the eyes of the eighteen guys seated around him on all sides. Glancing up, Chris noticed hydraulic fluid dripping down from a frame on the helo and smiled briefly as he recalled the words of an old Master Chief, "If it's not dripping, it ran out. Get ready to crash!" He breathed in the smell of JP5 (a kerosene-based jet fuel). That smell was a welcome friend.

The LZ, where the Team was headed that night, was "hot", meaning the Team expected a fight on landing—or earlier. Looking around him, especially at the much younger and newer SEAL team members, Chris soberly reflected, *We may not all be coming home tonight.* As the helicopter rotors hummed overhead, he reminded himself, *We have to do this job; our country expects it of us; we are the only ones who can do it. I volunteered.*

Chris saw that some of the young guys have fallen into a nervous half-sleep—the sleep the guys forced on themselves when the unknown overcame their mind's ability to grasp anything else but fear. Others stared at the floor, rehearsing the mission details in their head, over and over.

I'm the old guy, Chris reflected. He distracted himself by looking at a map, messing with the radio and checking last-minute details with the pilots. He knew he must not show anything on his face but steadfast determination and positive vibes. The younger ones looked to him for fortitude.

"Fifteen minutes out!" the helo crew chief called. The guys began to pass the word, one by one, everyone wide-awake now, checking their gear. A few guys did press checks (a quick check to ensure you are hot); most of the guys had been hot for months, the only time the round or a mag changed was in anger.

Looking around, Chris saw heads bobbing up and down to memories of Metallica or Hayseed Dixie, depending on where they grew up. Everyone was getting fired up, getting the blood going fast to make it possible to go from sitting down in the helo to a full-out sprint off the back into a hot landing zone.

"Five minutes!" the Chief called out. The green glows of the bobbing night vision glasses slowed down. Chris smiled, recognizing the ritual—everyone prays before a firefight—and he closed his eyes along with the others.

God guide me, he silently prayed, *Be with me, make me brave in the face of my enemy. Bless my guys all around me—bring us home. If I don't make it, take care of them. Take care of my two sons back in Minnesota—give them the peace I never had. Amen.*

Chris lifted his head. Some of the guys were still in their silent reprieve.

"One minute!" the chief called. *We're back to rock and roll!* Chris shouted inside his head as he stood with the others. Everyone gave one last gear check, stomped their feet, stretched. The helo started its final approach to a mark set by a special team who was already there.

The helo's crew chief yelled, "Get ready boys, same as we do every night! Fire it up! Everyone comes home!" The helo did a hard bank and then flared. The back ramp was down as they touched the ground. Everyone ran out into the desert night.

There was an explosion in the distance as everyone headed toward the opening in the wall that was just made by the breaching team. So far all was according to plan.

Good breach! Chris thought to himself as he ran for the opening where the wall crumbled under the blast. The breachers were wearing the garb of locals and had been ready for a while. It was hard to see, and it looked like chaos, but everyone was on the phase line and timed from launch.

Overhead, a Predator was tracking it all, announcing "BLUE PHASE LINE CLEAR" over the command channel seconds after the blast and sending live video feedback to Headquarters and to the commanders on the ground. On the feed, there was a phase line of aircrafts: 53s, little birds and an overhead AC130, all holding or circling to east of the compound. The little birds swung into their places and dropped off the roof teams. The other 53 is flaring hard and poured a line of figures from the back ramp—SOF Operators and a team of Afghan Commandos. As the newly-inserted warriors took their places, the line of figures running to the still-scorching hole in the wall began to enter the compound going to their targets.

Seeing everything through the green glow of NVGs, Chris ran with the team as they each took their positions and began clearing the center of the compound. Chris had moved into combat mode—totally detached from emotions and from his physical body. In this mode, he and the guys beside him seemed less like bodies and more like souls, fighting side by side—fighting other souls. Moving like a machine, Chris felt time slowing down as he entered a calm peace amidst the combat.[1]

As their team entered the center of the compound, he saw that the roof-top overwatch was clearing the roof. *Sleeping guys and guards, taken out or cuffed,* Chris thought as his eyes scanned the compound. Everyone had their place and the teams were moving in a highly-choreographed manner. Some were shooting Taliban in the compound while Chris's team cleared out to the right, shooting every armed man in sight. Chris had the backs of the three men in front of him: Jason, Kyle and Smitty—together they formed a four-man element and moved fast for the first buildings. They entered the first room, scanning and shooting.

Not according to plan, the rest of the force was somehow detained on the left side of the compound. And suddenly from an adjacent compound, a vehicle with a mounted DShK (Dish-Ka a Soviet heavy machine gun) abruptly smashed through a main entrance—a double garage-size door—and drove to the back of the compound. Angry Taliban began shooting toward the little birds and strafing the entire compound. The little bird blasted the Taliban combat truck and stopped it cold. There are a few other Taliban on foot who were awakened and join the fight.

On the Command Communication Network, they struggled to pinpoint the positions of the guys in the compound to prevent blue on blue. Chris listened to the command net as he and his group were separated and pinned down by the new force.

Chris and Jason gave cover; Kyle kneeled and set up charges on the adjacent wall and blasted through it, providing an escape. The four-man team entered through the hole blasted into the next room while women and children were pushed to the side and instructed not to move. They joined the rest of the team and continued the clearance.

Then, a big explosion. Chris's night vision goggles go black.

Later, Chris wakes up in a Helo.

Where's Smitty? He tried to form the words, but his lips wouldn't move. At the hospital, he was still not feeling in his body, flashing in and out in the operating room, flashing back into the fight. *Where is everybody? What happened? Where's Smitty? Jason? Kyle? What went wrong?*

Chris took some frag from the explosion and has a concussion—the blast knocked him unconscious but was told he should be fine. The doc at the firebase took care of the frag, only a few pieces—ready to rock and roll again.

"A few of the Afghan Commandos and John didn't make it," Jason later told him. John's body had already been sent home—stateside. To his wife and children.

It should've been me! Chris screamed in anguish inside his head upon learning the news. *Why do I stay alive when good family men like John dies? It should have been me!* he thought thinking at least if he had died there would be no more battles with trying to live a man's life while inside a transgender female.[2]

FIRST LIFE—THE HOME FRONT
1945-1991

Chris on the pond in back of their farmhouse.

Chris, Hanna and their Mom on their farm circa 1974.

Chris playing tennis in high school, 1983.

Chris in high school, 1983.

Chris riding his horse in a parade down Main Street in 1984.

WWII & Homecomings

"Welcome home Dad!" thirteen-year-old Luther (eventually to be Chris's father) called as his father, Samuel Beck, stepped out of the taxi in full uniform and swung his heavy bag up to the steps of their small home. The American flag was hanging proudly and Luther's mom, Judy, came running down the porch steps and embraced Sam with pure joy. Judy was wearing a blue and white cotton dress for the occasion with her hair held back in a blue ribbon and red lipstick lighting up her lips. The two kissed briefly and embraced tightly until the other three kids came running behind to greet their father.

Samuel had left three years earlier after enlisting to fight the Japanese after Pearl Harbor, leaving their mother pregnant with their fourth child. And now that the war was over he was home.

"I am grateful to be alive and back here with my family. I don't have anything to say about what happened over there." Sam told them from the couch that afternoon, refilling his glass of whiskey between stories before finally leaving to stare at the painted wall on the other side of the room. Over the years a few of the stories did spill out, stories of Sam fighting the Japanese, the Kamikazes' and the many loses he had in battles in the Pacific. But for the most part, like many veterans of war, Sam kept his pain bottled up and didn't let anyone in.

Previously, Sam hadn't been a smoker or a big drinker, but as the days went by, he smoked liked a chimney and liked to booze up all the time. Luther was happy that his father was home but confused at how changed he was. At his age, Luther didn't really understand that his father was fighting his demons—and losing.

Luther had carried a big load while his father was gone. His mother was still working as a nurse at the hospital taking care of the wounded soldiers, and often Luther was left at home to heat up a meal, clean up, or to watch over his siblings while she worked. Now everything was turned around: the war was ended, his father was home, his mother quit working, and he no longer had to be "the man of the house"—but nothing was the same and it certainly had not turned out for the better.

***

Months went by but the family did not reconstitute itself as they had once been. The wounds of war were too strong for that. Sam spent his days and nights sitting drinking and smoking on the couch in front of the television or out with friends. He lost jobs and found other work along the way.

On one of those nights Sam fell asleep while his wife and kids were in their bedrooms sleeping. It was only when the sofa was set fully ablaze that Sam woke up.

"Holy shit!" Sam yelled in panic as he stood up and began pulling the burning sofa across the living room toward the front door. As he brushed past the draperies, flames leapt from the sofa to the draperies and set them on fire as well.

Throwing open the door, Sam struggled to pull the sofa out the front door but he only succeeded in pulling it partway through—effectively blocking the main exit of their home, which was rapidly becoming an inferno.

Luther waking to the sounds of his father's shouting and smelling smoke in the air came running.

"Oh my God!" he called out as he raced toward the living room that was ablaze with no escape. Luther could see fire spreading from the sofa and draperies to the entire room and moving to the rest of the house.

I've got to save the others! Luther realized and ran to his mother's room and then to the other rooms. "The house is on fire!" he shouted, waking his brother Stevie and his sisters Linda and Betty. "Come, we need to go out the window! Over here!" Disoriented, his mother and siblings followed him through the smoke to the window. One by one Luther helped them climb out.

His father, still dazed from the smoke and burns he received from trying to wrestle the couch out of the house, was stumbling about in shock on the front lawn.

By this time the entire house was in flames—the heat and smoke were overwhelming. If he could turn back inside and run again through the flames to get his three-year-old sister Katie and make it back here safely, she'd be saved. But looking at the flames overtaking the room Luther realized, *There's no way. I have to get out, now!* Luther jumped out of the window to join his brother and sister. Katie died in the flames still in her crib.

Watching their home collapse in flames and realizing the loss of Katie, Sam stood in the front yard holding his wife and family weeping.

After the fire, Sam stopped drinking and found a job as the pool director of a prestigious country club. But he and Judy were devastated by what had happened. And Luther grew up with a hole in his soul. *He hadn't saved his sister.*

It didn't matter to him that the fire was not his fault—that he had saved his mother, brother and sister. He'd failed to save Katie.

Luther grew up to become a star football player. He made first string at the University of Miami in his freshman year and then made it to the New York Jets, passing their try-outs. His knees would blow out before he actually played for the Jets, so Luther would become a high-school football coach instead, mentoring thousands of football players, "sons" that he could save and lead into great lives. Yet he still carried the self-loathing inside from not having saved his sister, a haunting guilt that followed him into his marriage and new family. And like his father, he would drink to chase his demons away.

When Chris reflected back on this story he noted that years afterward Sam, his grandfather, known to Chris as "Granpa", was an amazing person—generous and kind-spoken.

"Granpa made peace with himself and God and from then on never drank again," Chris recalled. "He led Bible studies, taught swimming to the local kids and crusaded for the righteous and good until his death from a heart attack in 1985. Once he found his way again—after he overcame his war wounds and the fire—he was a very good man. He brought out the best in many people in his later life and he had heart of gold.

"I remember when we lived on the farm, Granma and Granpa would drive up from their home in Long Island for a visit, and he always brought with him a box of Dunkin Donuts," Chris recalled. "My mother always cooked from our garden and the farm—we never had store-bought treats— so for a boy like me, it was heaven!" Chris said smiling with the delightful memory crossing his mind.

"In the later years, my father and grandfather would take walks and sit by the pond out back and talk. I never saw my grandfather touch my dad— barely even a handshake—but they talked. I think it was mostly football and Jesus.

"My grandfather was a WWII veteran—he had stories—but he bottled them up and crushed them. I wish I could talk to him today," Chris reflected wistfully. "Give him a hug; tell him some of my stories of the Serb Drina Wolves, the Iraqi Republican Guard, al-Qaeda and the Taliban. The mistakes I made, the good, the bad.

I made it home—like he did. I wished I hadn't—like he did.

But now, I am trying to redeem myself and so something great with my life, like my grandpa did."

THE SIXTIES

In the United States, the late sixties was a time of great social change. On the domestic scene, Lyndon B. Johnson was in the White House following the assassination of John F. Kennedy in 1963. Martin Luther King, Jr. was leading the civil rights movement. He and Robert Kennedy were both assassinated two years later. On the international stage, the Six Day War broke out in June of '67 with the Israelis quickly becoming the overwhelming victors. The Vietnam War—with no clear victory in sight—was still grinding on. One hundred and ninety thousand troops were deployed, a number that would eventually rise to over three million American troops sent to Southeast Asia.

When Chris was almost one, the Beatles released their eighth studio album, Sgt. Pepper's Lonely Hearts Club Band, and later in that month they debuted their hit song "All You Need is Love" live on black-and-white television. And on the summer solstice of 1967, a year after Chris was born, over a hundred thousand people between the ages of fifteen and thirty gathered in San Francisco for the so-called "Summer of Love". The hippie movement, civil rights crusade and antiwar protests were all in full swing by the time Chris was a toddler.

Chris's parents were not part of that movement. In fact they were conservative Christians—Lutherans and later Evangelical Christians who believed sex was for the sanctity of marriage and that using recreational drugs was sinful. Chris's father, Luther, and his mother, Kate, believed in the inerrancy of scripture and called themselves evangelical fundamentalists. There was no modern re-interpretation of scriptures for them.

Luther taught at a local high school and worked as a football coach while he pursued another personal dream: owning a farm like John Wayne. This meant he rose early to feed the animals and milk the cows and then returned home from teaching all day to slop the pigs and clean out the horse stables.

Luther and Kate already had two children: four-year-old Hanna and two-year-old Jake. Having a daughter was great, but this time round, Luther was hoping for another son—if he was going to have a successful farm, he needed help to keep things running. And as the coach of the local high school football team, he also dreamed that maybe—if he couldn't do it himself—he could raise and train one of his sons to take over where his first dream of playing professional football fell short—a son who would not only make the cut, but would actually play on a professional team.

And in October of 1966, the DNA of his mother and father combined in the unique fashion that would form one distinct human being—with both an X and a Y chromosome, starting the exciting but perilous journey of becoming the infant who nine months later would be born and named Chris Beck.

Then, as now, scientists could not yet say how the bio-chemistry in the womb interacts with how genes express themselves within their environment, but if there had been the possibility back then to look into the womb, to read this unique human genetic code and see and portend the future, the teller of fate at that time would surely have said this is a *boy* and foretold that this baby was destined to become a *man*. We would soon see, however, that that would have told only half the story.

THE GREAT GENDER DIVIDE

"It's a boy!" the doctor declared in a joyful voice to Chris's mother and the attending nurses.

"I have another son!" Luther told his parents, his voice overcome with emotion as he spoke into the pay phone that he kept dropping quarters into. Luther had been anxiously pacing in the waiting room up to then waiting for the news.

Chris, too, had been waiting to be born. During the first two months of life in the womb, Chris's brain—like all other human beings at that initial stage of gestation—was female. But around eight weeks gestation, the brain begins synthesizing hormones and the physical body begins to form as male or female. Chris's brain started bathing his system in testosterone and organizing his cell division and anatomical development, so that at birth the doctor took one look at Christopher's young baby body and declared him male.

**

"Welcome Home!" the crayoned sign hanging over the door read as Luther drove baby Chris and his mother Kate up the driveway to their home from the hospital.

"Where's the baby?" Hanna asked as she and Jake ran up to the car to greet their new baby brother.

"Can I hold him?" Hanna begged as everyone gathered around. Gingerly Kate placed Chris, bundled in his blue blanket into Hanna's little arms while Luther hovered around shooting photos. The flashbulbs of his camera flashed brightly with each shot and then sizzled dead so that Luther had to remove and screw in a new flashbulb between each shot. Luther didn't often take photos, as funds were tight on his high school teacher's salary and it would cost additional money to develop them. But he took a few photos to memorialize the homecoming of his second son.

"We're hungry!" Luther said turning to his wife afterwards. Dutifully she walked up to their bedroom where she put the baby down in his cradle and took up her tasks again as wife and mother.

"The baby's crying," Hanna came to tell her many times a day.

"I'll get him in a minute," Kate answered, but often baby Chris had to wait as Kate had little time to coddle another child. Her hours were filled as she had to balance raising the children, doing the laundry, shopping and making the meals, as well as helping her husband run his farm. It was exhausting and she was always running at her limit.

"I can't wait until they are old enough to help me in the barn," Luther told Kate. "And to go hunting!"

Being traditional in his views, Luther held to a strict division of labor in his household: the boys would do the "male" tasks of running the farm, taking the garbage out, mowing the grass and shoveling snow while the girls would help their mother cook, clean and run their home. The next two babies were girls—born to the "other" team.

Chris had no idea he'd been born a boy. He had no gender identity at birth—only a slow growing awareness of how he was treated and expected to behave. As all children growing up into the multiple expectations placed upon them, Chris experienced himself through the "looking glass self", seeing himself through the eyes of others.

In his parents eyes he was most definitely a boy destined to become a man. He was dressed in dark colors—usually jeans, a t-shirt and Chuck Taylor sneakers. His childhood clothes were emblazoned with trucks and fireman, whereas his sisters wore pink and white ruffled things fashioned out of much more delicate and frilly fabrics. His hair was shaved in the short buzz cut, favored at the time and which his mother could shave herself to save money—leaving a velvety layer of hair that he and his sisters liked to run their hands along. Hanna by contrast wore her hair long and she sat patiently while their mother braided or drew her hair up into cute braids or pigtails that Kate tied off with colorful bows.

When Chris wanted to be part of the girl's rituals he was actively rebuffed.

"That's for girls, silly!" Hanna said, taking one of her small plastic barrettes out of Chris's pudgy hand after he tried to fasten it into his short hair. And when the four-year-old Chris burst into tears she didn't give it back.

"You don't need a barrette," his mother explained. "You're a boy!"

Chris asked questions about why and how he and Hanna were different, but he was always rebuffed with vague reasons. Given that their mother—and the church—never gave labels to their male and female body parts or explained anything sexual, these conversations became difficult and everyone avoided them. Chris found it difficult to formulate more questions. And he began to understand that there was more to the sexual and gender divide than he had yet sensed, *but it was not something that could be openly discussed in his family or anywhere for that matter.*

"Those aren't for you!" Hanna told Chris, laughing when he tried to play with her Barbie dolls. And taking them out of his small hands she explained, "You're a boy!" It became a constant mantra separating him from his sisters' lives, while Chris continued to circle back to try to join and understand.

"Boys don't cry," Luther told Chris and Jake from an early age. Luther didn't want the boys to grow up to be "sissies" and he was tough on them—more so on Chris.

"Pink is a girl color! You're a boy, not a girl!" Luther said, when Chris was fascinated with his sister's things and he firmly redirected his son away from any preference for the feminine.

"Boys don't paint their nails or look pretty!" Kate admonished, a look of disapproval crossing her face when Chris asked to be included when his sisters were getting their nails done.

"Go and get a football!" Luther said as he continued to teach the boys the ways of men. But when they played football with their father, Jake always managed to capture Luther's admiring attention, leaving Chris out of the limelight.

"Look at the way he catches!" Luther called out. "He's a natural born player!"

When Chris turned five, Luther began taking him along with Jake on the rounds, showing them both how to carry a water bucket for the animals, how to slop a pigsty. "Pour it out here," Luther directed. "Make sure you pitch all the dirty hay—don't leave any behind!"

Luther demonstrated and always expected his sons to pay attention, learn their chores fast and perform them at a high level. Luther had no patience for slacking off and quickly started counting to three when their attention wandered or the boys tried to turn things into a game. "Pay attention! This is important!" his father growled if Chris started playing around. Luther often shook Chris by jerking on the scruff of his jacket, and when the counting got to three, the belt came off.

Chris noticed that his father seemed to lose patience with him much easier than anyone else in the family—he seemed a bit of the lightening rod on which Luther often discharged his angry feelings. Even though he was still tough on Jake, he definitely had a softer spot for him. *It's because he's blonde and better at sports* Chris concluded. Luther also had an extremely soft spot for his sisters, rarely making any demands of them.

I want to be Hanna! Chris frequently wished. While he put on his little boots and a jacket early in the mornings braving the cold weather to go outside to shovel snow, or feed the farm animals; Chris saw that his sisters stayed inside and seemed to have a much nicer life helping their mother.

I'd rather be a girl and stay with them! They get to have all the fun. Chris thought to himself.

A Father's Payment Forward

"Tag you're it!" Hanna called out as she ran past Chris, tagging him on the back. It was cold outside and they were all stuck inside the house—bored. Hanna streaked off across the kitchen and into the living room shrieking, with Chris in hot pursuit. Jake ran along after and Karen, the fourth and newest child, soon joined in the fun of chasing around the room.

"You're it!" Chris shouted as he turned suddenly and tagged Jake. Jake chased Chris back across the room where they both ran, squeezing their bodies between the sofa and a small table. Laughing heartily neither boy noticed when one of their little legs caught the cord of a nearby lamp. As they cavorted onward, the lamp crashed to the floor, sending reverberations of the loud crash throughout the house.

"What idiot did that?" Luther roared as he angrily entered the room and saw the shards of the lamp laying about the floor. Hanna began to cry while Karen and Jake stood staring silently in fear at their father.

"Who did this? *Chris was it you?*" his father roared singling out the son he'd already long ago decided was the troublemaker. Luther saw the guilt on all their faces and he knew they were all to blame, but he never blamed the girls, and rarely—if ever—yelled at them, and Jake somehow always seemed more innocent than Chris. So as usual, Luther turned his anger to his second son.

"*Chris?*" his father demanded. Six-year-old Chris knew the drill. Jake would not be blamed, and Chris knew it was better to take the blame now then risk angering his father any further with hesitations.

"I broke the lamp," Chris said seeing the black fury building on his father's brow.

"Go and get the paddle," Luther directed, anger filling his voice. All the "*innocent*" children then scattered from the room with Chris walking heavyhearted toward the den where he lifted the paddle from its hook.

"You know this hurts me more than it hurts you!" Luther said as he hit Chris. "You need to learn to be responsible!" *You need to be a man!* Luther thought as he struck his son and unconsciously connected whatever he was punishing Chris for at that moment to his own serious—and never forgotten—failure in his own boyhood.

You can't be a screw-up! You can't be a failure! He knew he needed to teach his son early—make sure Chris learned it well and now. *Failure is not an option!*

None of his children could voice it at the time, but they learned over time, that Luther was incapable of expressing any serious blame to his daughters. Perhaps he was still heavy laden with the guilt that arose after having failed to save his own baby sister from the inferno that his father had caused so many years earlier. And when the shamed feelings of thirteen-year-old Luther standing outside of the house powerless to save his baby sister erupted again in scenes like this—where one of his sons had failed to protect home and hearth, Luther lost self-control, projecting his self-contempt without realizing he was doing so—upon Chris. , Luther felt that he had to make sure that his son would never be irresponsible, ill-prepared or such a slacker that he was not on top of his game. He could never let the past repeat itself—he had to teach Chris a lesson! "Chris will not fail. Chris will always be in front of the problem."[3]

In some ways it now seems to Chris like the Bible verse was being played out regarding "the sins of the fathers and the father's father being rained down upon the heads of their sons".

Little did Luther realize that in projecting his own childhood failure and self-condemnation on his own son in response to Chris's small and normal boyhood shortcomings, he was preparing Chris to someday become all that Luther feared he had *not* been. Luther was destining Chris to find his way to becoming the ultimate man, the ultimate rescuer, a Navy SEAL who would break all kinds of limits of endurance training. Chris would even become Honor Man in BUD/S training, pushing his body to the point of breaking to be number one and succeeding under the SEALs' and his father's mottos of *Do it right the first time—every time* and *Failure is not an option!*

Luther was barely conscious of his own inner workings. He would never actually think about that inferno years ago; he would just feel intolerable feelings of shame, anger and self-loathing and then rid himself of these intolerable feelings by projecting them entirely onto his son.

In his childhood, Chris couldn't see that this is what was *really* going on. Instead the father who wanted his son to *do better, be better and rise above* all the shame he felt deep inside was actually confusing the hell out of his son.

Why does he hate me? Why does he always blame me? Chris asked himself as he crouched in pain, tears welling up in his eyes while taking the blows. And after a paddling while running off in shame and anger to his bedroom, Chris would ask himself: *Why does he hit me? He never hits her! Why can't I be Hanna? She never gets in any trouble—he never gets angry with her! Why can't I be blonde and beautiful like Hanna, or blonde and athletic like Jake? I'm dark and ugly!*

As Chris grew older, he began to accept that it was he who was the "sinner" of the family, the black sheep, the one that was always getting called out and yelled at.

"You didn't slop the pigs!" his father would yell. "How could you forget to feed the horses?" And the paddle would come crashing down. And with each blow, deep inside Chris's psyche Luther was reinforcing all Chris's negative identification of himself as a boy—why would anyone want to be a boy if this is what it entailed?

SAFE PLACE

It was Saturday afternoon and all the men were headed out to the neighborhood bar. Luther left the boys in the car. "Don't get in trouble, I'll only be gone for a couple of drinks."

"Let's get out of here," Jake said as soon as their dad disappeared inside the bar. Unlocking the doors, the boys warily scrambled out of the car and ran off a ways from the bar where they began scouting for bottles and cans. When they had collected enough they made their way on foot alongside the highway to the general store.

"Good job, boys," the old man who owned the place praised them while taking their bottles and cans and allowed them to trade for a couple of cans of soda pop—Grape Nehi was Chris's favorite. Drinking their sodas on the way back to the car, the boys always made sure to be inside the car before their father emerged from the bar to drive them home. Chris was at risk if something went wrong after a weekend of Luther's drinking.

On those days, if Chris screwed up—which he often did as any normal child would, Luther paddled Chris harder than he should have while saying, "You know this hurts me more than it hurts you!"

But hours later—after seeing the welts he had caused, Luther would realize that perhaps he had hit his son harder than he should have and had hurt Chris more than he meant to. At those times the shame might drive Luther to go out the next day to buy Chris a small gift that he nonchalantly gave his son without an apology. It would always be a boy toy: a fishing reel, a special pen or a wristwatch; the things Luther didn't get as a boy and wanted.

Chris rejected those gifts. And each time he singled out his son out to *Be a man!*, Luther drove Chris farther and farther away from that goal, strengthening his desire to somehow switch bodies with his sister, which Chris believed could perhaps end all this sadness and self hatred. In bed at night Chris would fervently pray to the Baptist God who he had learned (at the Christian school his parents had now enrolled him in) was all seeing and all-powerful:

Please God let me change bodies with Hanna. Please let me wake up in her body! Can't you change me? And save me?

Of course those prayers were never answered because the Baptist God is quite strict about such things—changing one's birth-assigned sex is not allowed and even very vocally condemned as a grave and horrific sin. Chris didn't realize that as a young boy.

He was not even consciously aware, but during all those years of his early childhood Chris's mind was responding to extreme stress and anxiety, and deep inside some extremely important gender related decisions were being made: on an unconscious level he was concluding that it was not safe to be a boy, especially a son in his family. The load of self-hatred projected upon him by his father—because of Luther's own childhood trauma—was too heavy of a load to bear and Chris was responding by learning on the deepest levels of his core self that it was much better to be a girl.

Please let me wake up in Hanna's body! He continued to beg God at night, yet his body did not change.

Chris found another way to comfort himself. He began to steal Hanna's clothes and dress his male body up to match his inner girl. . . The first time was before kindergarten; Hanna dressed him in a little purple ballerina outfit. He felt happy and safe. Now in grade school, he would sneak into Hanna's room to dress up. This was an escape from his father's premature demands to be a man—demands that he wasn't sure he could ever meet.

As time went on he developed a habit of taking Hanna's clothes and then late at night when no one could catch him doing it, he put them on. Dressed in her clothes he got back under the covers to sleep as a girl—to be safe, to be his sister who was loved, pampered and protected by everyone. Mentally he slipped out of his male body and escaped the body that kept getting blamed, paddled and had to do all the work. The comfort of it was overwhelming.

Of course that meant he had to be the first awake to slip back out of his "nice" clothes before anyone saw him. Later he would add even more elaborate schemes for hiding his self-comforting rituals. He had to—the need deep within his soul took him over completely. He would become a girl—he was a girl!

MISBEHAVING

"Grab the desk," Chris's first grade teacher instructed. He'd done it again—jumpy and uncomfortable in his own skin, Chris had gone too far. And now he was feeling the crack of the wooden paddle whacking hard down on his backside. The class watched from their desks in silence as they always did. Many of them never misbehaved just from the site of Chris getting the paddle.

Chris was often making wise cracks that he—but no one else—seemed to think were funny. It seemed like he was getting the paddle almost everyday.

Already in first grade, Chris knew he was an underdog, a misfit—a child that couldn't behave right, that couldn't win the approval of those who mattered—his parents and teachers at school. He kept getting hit by them and the pain of it—emotional and physical—fueled his desire to continue escaping his body, escaping this world.

At dinner, Chris's mother, Kate, would set a beautiful table and gather flowers from her garden in a big vase that she set at the table. When she served the meal Luther instructed Chris to sit across from him at the dinner table, hidden from sight by the vase of flowers.

"Sit there where I don't have to see you and your terrible manners," Luther said in his stern voice. "I hate the way you chew with your mouth open and forget how to use your fork properly, Stop fidgeting! Sit still!"

As they ate their meal, Chris glanced over at Hanna and tried to imitate how she used her fork gracefully and took small bites like a proper young lady. *I can be like her and be good*, Chris thought to himself, knowing inside that he was a girl.

Over the next few years, Luther would take the boys outside and drill them in sports. It seemed to Chris as though Jake could throw strike pitches before Chris even learned to pick up the ball. And in football Jake also excelled, winning their father's prideful enthusiasm. Soon Luther was grooming Jake to play quarterback. Envying his blonde, naturally athletic brother, Chris continued to feel cast aside by his father. He would try harder and practice hours on end to catch up—but this extra effort was never noticed.

***

"What is it?" Chris asked as he unwrapped his Christmas gift in third grade.

"It's a ski-sled," his father answered smiling and as Chris examined it he saw that the wood was shaped in the form of a long narrow toboggan with a long rope attached on the front and could indeed be used to sled—only it required standing up.

Taking it out back on the snowy but uncleared hill on the other side of the pond that afternoon, Chris forced himself to try and balance on it as he struggled to steer it down the hill in between protruding rocks and small brush. It took him the whole afternoon and into the evening before he finally navigate the entire hill and ski on it without losing his balance.

"You're one hard-headed kid," Chris's mother said shaking her head in disbelief, rather than praising his determination when he came in to announce his victory. His cheeks were glowing red and he was obviously proud of himself, but her words took the wind out of his sails.

Chris took off his jacket and boots, placing them carefully on the plastic mat provided to catch the melting slush and went to his room. There he pulled out a pair of Hanna's tights from his hiding place in the back of his closet and removing his jeans he slipped them up over his legs feeling the calm sense of his female self overtaking him.

OBSESSION

Dressing up and "becoming" a girl soon took on a life of its own and doing it only at night was not enough. The delight Chris felt in being a girl overcame him totally and he began risking dressing in Hanna's clothes in his room or under his boy clothes during the day as well.

One day Luther happened into his room when Chris was playing quietly wearing one of Hanna's skirts.

"What the hell are you doing wearing that dress?" Luther shouted dumbfounded at the sight. He scooped up Chris in a rage and shook him hard. "Take that off right now! "I don't ever want to see you doing something so perverse as that again! Boys do *not* wear dresses! You got that?" he shouted.

Chris got the message. He tried hard many times to stop, but in the end always found himself compelled to do it. If he wanted to live in his "safe space", he needed to do it under the radar. He was a girl--but he knew better than to ever act or dress the part amongst his family members or anyone in this world.

Trying to follow a strict Baptist interpretation of Christianity, Chris's whole family was sexually repressed. No one had taught any of the kids about the "birds and the bees"—these topics were learned at school in class or from other kids. The only clear messages were, *we don't talk about sex* and *sex is bad!* Private parts were not named or mentioned.

"We were all repressed in our tight roles, like champagne bottles all corked up and then shaken," Chris recalled.

Intent on making sure Chris would take the straight and narrow, Luther continued to use the paddle often. The reasons varied: it could be he didn't slop the pigs right, wasn't careful about throwing the hay bales, forgot a chore, didn't do it quickly or correctly, broke something or teased the girls. There seemed no end to reasons to paddle the "bad" out of Chris. Chris found that the only time he got attention or was touched by anyone was when he was getting punished.

As Christmas rolled around in fourth grade, Chris noticed that his father's rejection also filtered into the gift giving.

"Oh, they're beautiful!" Hanna exclaimed pulling shiny black patent leather shoes from a box as she threw the decorated Christmas wrap to the side. Chris looked on as Hanna, Kate and Karen opened up box after box of beautiful girl gifts: locket necklaces, frilly dresses, pretty shoes, girl toys—all things his mother had likely picked out. Then when his turn came Chris opened a box with a navy blue sweater inside, feeling sullen as he watched Jake tear the gift-wrap off a Daisy Red Ryder BB gun.

The family was challenged financially, although that didn't explain the seemingly unfairness of how the gift giving went. *They must have spent twenty dollars on Hanna and only a few on me!* Chris thought to himself as hurt and anger welled up inside. As Jake took his new BB gun out of its box and began to examine it, tears stung behind Chris's eyes but he was too afraid of his father to cry.

Boys don't cry! He remembered his father's words as he struggled to keep his feelings inside. He slipped out of the living room and went upstairs to put on a pair of hose underneath his pants and returned to the family. It felt so much better to at least have something nice on while living in this fog.

After another move to a new house, Chris convinced his parents to let him build out the attic for his bedroom. It was his castle—a private Idaho with his own door and stairwell fortified to keep out intruders—and a place where Chris began to develop his own variant of "covert CIA operations or tradecraft". He became good at compartmenting pieces of his life and keeping everything organized and marked to see changes; these skills would pay off well in the job of his future.

Cleverer than his teachers realized, Chris had a good mechanical sense and he quickly understood how to position mirrors in the room so that he could quickly see anyone coming before they got to his room. And using his lawn mowing earnings, Chris became a favorite at Radio Shack, learning how to put up a sensor and light to alert him of any intruders before they were too close to his room so that Chris could switch out of his girl's wear.

Chris had amassed a small collection of clothes in his attic room that he had filched from his sisters. At night, as he sat doing his homework he would dress himself as the girl he had become.

I'm a girl, Chris would say to himself while still seeing the painful truth: he was still stuck in a boy's body and his female self that would never be accepted by God, his family or the world, as he knew it, but at least he could have some peace and comfort when in isolation.

FINDING GOD—HELL & BRIMSTONE

While Chris was in middle-school, his parents "found God" in the teachings of Southern Baptist preacher Jerry Falwell, a man who would later go on to establish the so-called "Moral Majority, a group that mobilized Christian conservatives to become politically active fighting against legalized abortion and gay rights. Joining the Baptist church, Chris's parents added another layer to their already conservative Lutheran backgrounds.

"The kids need a conservative Christian education," Luther told his wife. "I've been offered a job in a Baptist school in Virginia." They both agreed it was a good idea to pull their kids out of the local secular schools and move. They didn't want their children to be exposed to the liberal and sinful ways that seemed to be sweeping over the country in the late sixties and early seventies.

So eschewing the public schools where sex education and liberal ideas were taught, Luther took the job at Lynchburg Christian School where he would teach and coach football and where all his children could be enrolled.

As Chris holed himself up in increasing isolation, asking himself, *Why can't I be a girl? I don't know why, it's just the way I feel. I try not to feel this way; I try to be like Jake, but I can't. I'm a girl!* Luther was also going through a deep transition. Having "found religion" and realizing that his drinking was out of control, he began attending AA meetings and resolved to sober up. He concentrated on his football team, his gifted athletes whom he called his "sons", and the team that eventually went undefeated and gained titles and accolades throughout the East coast. This also made him even more intolerant of anything Chris was up to.

Now, attending Jerry Falwell's church with his family, Chris quickly discovered that his fellow congregants, including his classmate Jonathan Falwell, were completely intolerant of anything he felt inside. As puberty hit and Chris was going through his own gender identity struggles—a struggle he could not speak to his parents about because sex was not talked about in his home, Chris found himself increasingly at the mercy of a God who didn't seem to be a God of love.

Stories of hell and brimstone were told and examples of a busy, demanding, judgmental, physically cold and punitive God were modeled for Chris when he was taught in his Christian elementary school to consider the love of God to be like that of his own father. Chris recoiled inside knowing that his father would beat the hell out of him if he knew about his "inner girl".

As Chris became more aware he also came to understand that in his church of the Baptist God, the "sins" that were more commonly practiced by the congregants than any of them would ever openly admit to. Marital infidelity, pornographic use, abortion, premarital relations, and more were often buried deep in layers of secrets and hidden under coatings of highly polished church-going veneer. And to keep the focus off their own anxiety ridden sinful souls, the congregants delighted in pointing out and condemning the "sins" that were not so commonly practiced among the "saved"—"sins" such as homosexuality or, God forbid, transexuality.

As Jerry Falwell stated,

> "AIDS is the wrath of a just God against homosexuals. To oppose it would be like an Israelite jumping in the Red Sea to save one of Pharaoh's charioteers . . . AIDs is not just God's punishment for homosexuals; it is God's punishment for the society that tolerates homosexuals."[4]

The good Baptists found it was always reassuring to point to the sins of *others*, while claiming it's not us that are sinning against our great, glorious, loving and punitive God! *It's the homosexuals and the transgender people!* Chris knew to silence himself among these who would so quickly condemn him as well.

Chris thought, *If only this God and his followers would live in compassion to all those made in "His" image, wouldn't there be peace and fellowship among all people?* Chris wondered as he began to learn more. *This God created me and inter-sexed people, hermaphrodites and many other variations in the human species. Are we not all humans made in His image? If we all showed some respect and compassion for everyone, there would be so much less sadness and self-abuse. Can't we just have forgiveness and compassion?*

Zen & the Art of Living in the Woods with a Motorcycle

Luther's motorcycling days lasted for years but ended abruptly when he ran at high speed into a dog running across the road. The crash totaled the motorcycle and almost killed Luther. After that, Luther gave up motorcycling and Kate would never stand to see anyone in her family wrecked this badly again. But when Chris got a part-time doing construction worker with a contractor in high school, it was there—in the corner of the garage of Nick Burns, the contractor he worked for—that Chris saw his dream: an old Honda motorcycle. Freedom.

"I'll take that motorcycle in the corner instead of a paycheck," seventeen-year-old Chris said one day after a long day's work. He nodded to a burned out and dusty motorcycle in the corner hoping Nick would agree.

"I should throw it out, but I keep thinking about getting it fixed," Nick answered.

"I can fix it," Chris offered, although he'd never actually put his hands on a motorcycle.

"Okay. At the end of the pay period it's yours," Nick said, smiling silently at the kid's hutzpa. *He'll never get it running,* Nick thought shaking his head as he walked away.

But his childhood on the farm had given him a mechanical edge, as well as an engineering proclivity that Chris had found was the only thing his father supported, and after work Chris borrowed Nick's tools and began taking the bike apart and reworking it. It took him a month but he got it running. Then he shined it up and rode it home—proudly cruising down the family's driveway proudly.

"You'll not live in this house with that motorcycle!" his mother shouted. She wasn't about to let her son—especially her wild son—crash his motorcycle, too. She was sure he'd kill himself.

"Fine, then I'll live somewhere else!" Chris answered as he packed up some blankets and some warm clothes and angrily got on his motorcycle and rode away. It was late Fall and there was some snow on the ground in upstate New York. Chris had no idea where to go but he was sure of one thing: he was going to keep his motorcycle.

Riding it up the hill on the country road away from the house, Chris decided to camp in a forested area under some pine trees not far from a halfway house for troubled boys, Gil's Hills. Parking his bike, Chris took out his knife and slashed branches off the trees and then built himself a lean-to. *I can sleep here, I just have to find a place to get food and a shower,* he thought.

"Can I work here? Wash dishes and clean up for you in return for my meals and a place to study in the evenings?" Chris asked Gil, the owner of the halfway house. When Gil agreed, Chris felt set for surviving the harsh winter elements. His blankets and the mound of pine needles would keep him warm, he got meals and warm place to study at night, high school during the days and a shower after wrestling practice everyday. This would be his routine and new home for the next two months until his father came to bring him home—with the motorcycle and no more arguments from his mother.

JAKE'S MEAN SPIRITED JOKE

Jake, always the natural athlete and already the favored son, was given the coveted position of quarterback on the football team the following fall, while Chris always tenacious and unwilling to give up was the nose guard.

Luther was a tough coach and kept a paddle from the previous Christian school in the locker room. That paddle was a flatly shaved baseball bat with ten holes drilled into it. Luther would lecture his team about the last school and give lessons that were learned the hard way. "Cleanliness is next to godliness!" he would reiterate, warning that if anyone left anything smelling in their locker or a bad mess the offender got a paddling. Chris got such a paddling just once—in ninth grade at the old school. That story was repeated and the others quickly learned not to test this offense.

The fear of the paddle, however left Chris with a lifelong compulsion: he'd feel anxious when things got dirty or messy and feel strongly compelled to clean or straighten as his father's angry demands, still lingering in his head, would get the best of him. But sometimes he'd also he'd push back with anger. *Oh fuck it!* he'd think as he got a certain satisfaction in failing to clean or straighten up—until the anxiety always built and he finally cleaned up.

"You've got a weird sense of justice," Chris's mother remarked when he came home one day from high school with a black eye after fighting off some guys picking on someone. She was commenting on the fact that Chris would stand up for the underdog even to the "point of your own demise," as she put it. What she didn't realize was that after being the underdog or scapegoat in his father's eyes for so many years, Chris had an acute sense of empathy for anyone who was unfairly picked on.

For his part, Jake learned early on how to play upon Chris's sense of justice and often would complain to Chris about things he found unfair, including their father's demands to complete chores. If he got Chris burned up enough about it, Jake could count on Chris to be the one to complain— ensuring that Chris got his father's wrath and Jake got by unscathed.

Jake, although the favored son—at least in Chris's view of the situation—had his own issues. He wasn't as good a student as Chris and perhaps because he let Chris do the majority of the work, he felt jealous of Chris's abilities. To take out his emotions Jake would often passive aggressively get at Chris by joking around, teasing him at school, or by causing "accidents", like "accidentally" hitting Chris above his eye socket with a pitchfork or "accidentally" throwing Chris's favorite cowboy hat in the pigsty.

In high school Chris was socially awkward—perhaps not knowing how to relate as a boy to the opposite sex given that he was already gender identified as a female. He didn't feel gay either—he wasn't sure about anything—so Chris mostly shut down any sense of sexuality preferring to relate to others in a non-sexual manner. He tried to date girls and did a few times, but mostly it didn't work out. He mostly just wanted to be around the girls and be in the talks and gossip with them. He liked to be near them to see their clothes and wish he was wearing what they were wearing. He was an odd ball and an underdog.

Standing up for the other underdogs also didn't endear him to the "cool" kids. Chris played secondary roles in the theater and was generally a quiet student; he scored very high on the IQ test but he didn't try very hard and was bored. He goofed off a lot, though learned in elementary school through daily paddling that his sense of humor in the classroom was not appreciated. Jake, by contrast, was the high school quarterback and had only "cool" kids as his friends. But Jake had been held back in sixth grade, and so he and Chris were in the same class—although never in the same studies because Chris excelled in honors classes while Jake did not.

And on the football field, Chris was making strides, setting the year's record for the most quarterback sacks. Chris was the smaller of the two brothers, but he was genuinely tough and when he set out to punch through the line he'd do so with reckless abandon—willing to sacrifice his entire body to get to his goal. Jake lacked that kind of resolve and glided on his abilities without working at it.

Knowing that Chris was heading for the military and had been accepted to Virginia Military Institute (VMI), Jake's ultimate and final mean joke in high school was to arrange for the caption "Most likely to get killed by his own troops," from the movie "Animal House," to be printed under Chris's photo in their high school yearbook. When Chris saw it, he was devastated and still to this day stings over this insult from Jake and the cool "main street boys".

Virginia Military Institute

"No ordinary college. No ordinary life" is how the Virginia Military Institute (VMI) advertises itself. Indeed it's known for its "mission to prepare educated, honorable, and steadfast leaders" through physical, mental and leadership challenges. Chris attended school with an electrical engineering (EE) major, following in the tradition of his maternal grandfather, who had been an electrical engineer working for NASA.

"Here you will develop vision, discipline and strength—and you will reach beyond your perceived limits. If you put your minds to it you will face the joy of challenge and the shine of success. Our mission is to prepare educated, honorable and steadfast leaders in a diverse and dynamic world," the Commandant said at their opening day. "It means something to be here. It means something to push yourself further than you thought you could go."

Chris was attracted to the military system at VMI hoping it would prepare him for a life in the military—a life he was sure would win his father's approval and that hopefully would keep his "female" self at bay. Chris had been learning to deep-six this part of himself using suppression and denial, and being busily challenged at VMI would help with that. Cadets followed a military framework, wore uniforms dating back before the civil war, lived in barracks and ate their meals in mess halls like the regular military. Their days were strictly regimented with academic, military and physical training requirements. It was tough and demanding and after being raised by a father who was the same, Chris felt comfortable with that.

And Chris was ready to push to the limits. The only thing was, he was fighting an inner battle that required him to be always proving himself—especially to his father by excelling in sports. But at VMI, Chris had to succeed in academics and he needed help aligning his priorities correctly. Chris was in the ranger platoon and, even though he never played lacrosse in high school, he made the lacrosse team at VMI and soon after made it to the varsity lacrosse team. Chris and Ron Maass, another new lacrosse player, responded to the honor by single-mindedly practicing daily for hours at a time. Chris was forgetting that doing well and graduating with a major in electrical engineering might be more profitable to him in the long run than mastering lacrosse and being a second string player. Eventually in his junior year, sports won out over grades, and Chris was forced to transfer to Alfred University and change his major as well, to political science. There, Chris joined a fraternity and excelled in his classes.

THE FIRST TIME

Though Chris went into puberty on time and suffered a few wet dreams like all boys, perhaps because of his conservative upbringing and gender confusion he didn't have sexual intercourse until age twenty-two. It was at college in a small apartment above the local diner.

"I've never done this before," Chris told Angie as she began taking his shirt and then his jeans off.

"Don't worry, I'll show you everything," Angie said and she proceeded to do just that pushing Chris down on the bed while she climbed on top.

The second time they got together she asked, "How did you like it last time? Anything you want to do differently?"

Smiling Chris answered, "I loved it. Would you mind if I wore your pantyhose this time, while we do it?"

"Sure," Angie answered, a look of confusion and horror crossing her face, but they were already naked and she'd had a few drinks. *What's with this guy?* she thought to herself while squelching her "weirdness" monitors while they went ahead—Chris wearing Angie's pantyhose pulled up to his thighs.

Pretending he was the girl, Chris laid down and let Angie get on top and ride him again. Even though it was he penetrating her, her body thumping down on top of him gave him the sensation of being the girl. When they finished it was clear she understood what was going through his mind, and it was obvious—even though she was silent about it—that she wasn't pleased. That was the end of that relationship. Nearly the same would happen with all Chris's relationships for the rest of his life: awkwardness, then isolation and finally failure.

Chris was at Alfred University, a "very liberal" liberal arts college, famous around the world for ceramic engineering. There were artists who had a very free and fabulous life style; they did what they wanted and lived their own style. Compared to how Chris had grown up, this was like a different world. It was the first time Chris had ever really met any gay people. He joined a few of the pottery classes as his electives. He became a very good artist, throwing many pots and creating quite a few sculptures. He had found his calling? Maybe.

He had his private room and dressed when he could and became friends with many of the artists. He also played rugby and joined a fraternity. He enjoyed his time at Alfred and the freedom it presented. But he was still torn between the life he was living on the outside and the life he retained on the inside; he was living two lives and was afraid.

SECOND LIFE—NAVY SEALS

Chris as a young SEAL team guy in Panama.

Surf Passage in BUD/S.

Chris showing his BUD/S Swim Record.

After finishing the seven mile swim.

SEAL Diving Operations in 1995.

Chris in the 90s doing ship boarding.

Chris in 1999 on the Quarterdeck of the Naval Special Warfare
Command HQ with his 1960 Harley.

Shelly and Max watch Chris as he makes Chief in September 2000.

"Welcome Home." Chris and his boys in 2002.

Chris with his sons.

"Me and my boys relaxing together."

Boats at Basrah Palace after the UAV flights.

Chris holding Saddam's gold AK in Iraq.

Chris in Saddam's palace in Iraq.

Chris and Karl Borjes—"At the laboratory, building a new automated mortar system."

Chris in Iraq in April, 2003.

Chris with team guys in Iraq in April, 2003.

Chris with the 66FL he built himself.

Chris with parents, winning a prize for his motorcyle.

"Bourbon" helps Chris set gear.

Chris with "DJ" in Chamkani.

Chris and his Team under the "bones" after an operation in Afghanistan.

Chris at Bagram 2010.

Gun Trucks.

Chris in Afghanistan.

Chris in his uniform of the day in Afghanistan.

Chris with the locals in Afghanistan.

Chris with Mujahdeen Commander.

Chris attending the Shura in Afghanistan.

Chris on "standby" in Afghanistan.

Chris out on the range "confirming my dope in the back of our base in Afghanistan."

Chris on bike in Afghanistan.

"My Dad receives my medal while I'm in Afghanistan."

Chamkani Patrol.

Parachuting.

Chris and Samantha at a wine tasting.

CALL TO DUTY & DESERT STORM

After college, Chris got an analytic job in Washington, D.C. "What are you doing here wasting your life away?" Larry, Chris's much older work colleague, asked. "Look at you! You're smart, young, physically fit. Why not go for some adventures now when you can! This work is for retired guys—not you," Larry chided.

"What are you suggesting I do?" Chris asked, looking up at Larry from the stack of folders on his desk.

"You should look into the Navy SEALs! I think you could do it," Larry answered, smiling at the younger version of himself. Coming from Larry that was incredible encouragement—he'd been a Navy SEAL for almost thirty years.

"This desk job is my second time around. You shouldn't be doing this now at your age. Come back here when you're fifty years old like me!" Larry scoffed. "Go be a SEAL or some other job when you are young and fit! The country needs you; Desert Shield just kicked off. Watch the news!"

Still upset with his failure at VMI and what he perceived as his loss of a distinguished military career, Chris was encouraged to finally see himself positively in the eyes of a respected elder. He went down the very next day to the recruiting station and signed himself up for the U.S. Navy—fully intending to carry out Larry's vision of an adventurous future.

***

Chris went to boot camp and Quarter Master "A" school then finally made the journey to Coronado to start SEAL training with his buddy John, a legacy Navy man who knew exactly what he was getting into from his father, the Admiral. Chris only had a few stories of SEAL training and was mostly flying blind but was motivated to the core to make this his new life.

On the white sandy beach of Coronado Island at BUD/S training, Chris participated in the six-month grueling course to qualify as a "Basic Combat Diver", as well as an additional six months of advanced training which fully qualified one as a Navy SEAL.[5] Chris was completely determined to earn that trident—gritting up to his own personal limits—and then pushing even further. The inner female was completely suppressed—this was all about proving himself and regaining his sense of honor after having failed out of VMI.

After one of their runs when Chris had pushed himself beyond all normal human limits—finishing first in the four-mile run made in combat boots, full uniform and on the sandy beach, he buckled over puking on the cold Coronado Island beach.

"Twenty-four minutes!" the trainer called out. Finishing that fast made Chris an unusual outlier. The requirement for the run was thirty-two minutes. Most of the guys just made it in around twenty-nine minutes, but many didn't make it all and were sent to the "goon squad", where they had to do extra work and get tougher, faster, stronger.

The goon squad would still be running as the others did a warm-down stretch. If a trainee was gooned too many times, his body would break down and he would wash out. Many guys ended up this way and broke bones and their bodies trying to make it. And most of the guys were top athletes—there was even one Olympian athlete that washed out. Chris's friend, John, eventually washed out of the program due to slow run times.[6]

Failure is not an option! Chris kept the SEALs motto front and center as he pushed himself. *There've been too many failures!* Chris reflected when he had time to think, which was not often during training, and he was determined to succeed—to win his way into this family of "brothers" while he pushed the inner female down into the depths of his being.

Chris continued to finish number one or in the top few during every evolution throughout BUD/S. It hurt like hell and then some, but he understood that if you had the physical ability, if you were decently athletic and trained, which he was, the most important thing for making the BUD/S cut was the mental—keeping your head in the game, pushing your body past the limits. In fact, Chris was in such pain in his emotional life and because he didn't like the body he was stuck in, punishing it by pushing it beyond normal human limits was not only okay, but actually helped him to shove all else out of consciousness. Except perhaps, the knowledge that becoming a SEAL would finally earn his father's love and admiration. Ultimately, failing at this truly was not an option for Chris—he felt that he'd failed his father too many times and Chris could not take one more failure.

***

"Fifteen minutes!" The instructor yelled. The trainees were drown proofing, a carry over from Vietnam created when a captured SEAL ditched over the side of the Viet Cong sampan he was being carried away in, but drowned. In the drown proofing evolutions the trainees had their hands and feet tied up and then had to survive in the deep water, bobbing up and down in the water for thirty minutes followed by a lap swim to prove they were "drown proof" and wouldn't panic in the water—no matter what.

Surrounded by the others now bound and thrown into the deep end of the pool, Chris along with everyone else, struggled filling their lungs with water as they sank and managing somehow despite being tied up, to break the surface long enough to gulp down air, rather than water—repeating this again and again.

Out of the corner of his eye Chris realized that someone was drowning next to him. Suddenly an instructor appeared out of nowhere and yanked the drowning student out of the water. *He's unconscious!* Chris realized as he barely glanced out of the corner of his eye, struggling not to drown himself. He watched the instructor try to revive his classmate on the deck. *What if he doesn't come to?* Out of the corner of his eye Chris kept glimpsing fragments of this action as he managed to finish the evolution.

There in the pool Chris was already learning to enter his detached combat mode, watching everything—even himself—from a removed place in his mind, a place where hardly any emotional signals could break into consciousness: no fear, no anger, nothing but complete and total resolve. But as he would find as his SEALs career unfolded, the emotions he was able to dissociate from during combat didn't just disappear—they came later, often at the least expected times.

***

"Hey, your mother and I would like to come for a visit," Chris's dad had said over the phone soon after Chris made the SEAL teams. "I put a SEAL Team One sticker on the car," Luther continued enthusiastically.

So I finally count for something! Chris thought to himself—that is, when he had time to think. The SEALs training and fast turnarounds overseas didn't leave much time for personal reflection and even less time for family visits.

It was funny how once he was a SEAL many people took interest—not that it meant much to Chris. He and his SEAL brothers were kept busy most of the time; there was no time to think, to feel the pain or inner thoughts of his true self, and unfortunately no time now to spend with his now-proud father. That song always seemed to come true about the "Cats in the cradle..."

***

No matter how much he trained and succeeded in the SEALs—perhaps one of the manliest professions in the world, the inner female didn't entirely disappear. Sometimes the longings to make fully feel the inner woman were too much to suppress.

Chris made his first purchases of female clothing in San Diego, knowing he would be immediately kicked out of the SEALs if his sexual proclivities were discovered. Taking the clothing back to his room, he dressed up only in privacy, where he longingly admired and experienced himself as a woman before quickly disposing of these furtive purchases. He continued to buy clothes and keep them for a little while then totally purge his life of his femme attire.

Chris wished he could also shave his body, but there was no way he could do that in the SEALs except for once in a while when he had a rash or some other good excuse for it. Chris knew it was dangerous to have female clothing so he never kept his girl clothes for more than a few weeks and sometimes only for a few days. After expressing and appreciating himself in girl clothes, he'd throw everything away and vow never to do it again.

Frogman Luck

It was late at night and Chris and his team—Jonny, Cowboy and Sammy—were in a combat rubber raiding craft (CRRC) off of the island (in an undisclosed location). They had just swum in to the beach and placed explosives that were timed to explode any minute. Whenever they were on these missions and operating under threat, Chris felt a deep sense of camaraderie with his teammates, a spiritual brotherhood where animal instinct to survive and protect one another took over.

Even though he was functioning in what our society defines as a highly masculine role as a SEAL, for Chris it was in these SEAL activities when he most often detached from any sense of male or female—the threat was so high and the demands for his attention had to be one thousand percent on the tasks at hand.

Later when they would go into battles together, Chris found this sense of detachment with his mind and body deepening even more—the focus could only be on the battle, and things like sex were nearly wiped out. This detachment from the physical self sometimes even made Chris feel that they were all disembodied—just spirits fighting side by side against other spirits.

Now here late at night, after placing their explosives, the three SEALs swam back to the boat and laid down inside it on the tubes or on the floor boards, bored and waiting for the explosives to go off.

Suddenly Jonny, the coxswain, fired up the motor and started the boat moving ever so slowly.

"Why are you moving the boat?" Chris asked in a low voice.

"Ugh the exhaust fumes are killing me!" Cowboy hissed under his breath.

"Yeah, why are you jerking us around?" Sammy joined in. "Cut the motor! The fumes, What the fuck!!"

"Wait for the countdown!" Cowboy ordered.

Giving in to their complaints Jonny cut the motor. The boat had moved only five yards.

Five, four, three, two, one, zero the guys counted along mentally when Jonny started to laugh at Cowboy for missing the timing: "Ha, you cut the time-fuse wrong, fucker!" *One, two, three, four, five...*

"Shit!" Chris swore and asked Cowboy, "What did you do for the secondary initiator? The same length of fuse or was it that new TDFD (timed delay firing device)?"

Boom! The explosion answered his question and it was a much bigger than anyone expected. The beach imploded with rock and debris that began flying all over the place.

Suddenly one of the guys yelled as he stared at a giant boulder headed straight for them, which whizzed just past the boat and smashed into the water where their boat had sat only seconds before the coxswain had irrationally decided to move it. The boulder was bigger than the boat and sent the boat almost end over end.

"Seriously our boat was right there!" Jonny said, half laughing and half shitting himself.

Silently the guys stared at their lucky miss, realizing how closely they had come to death—and then everyone suddenly broke out in cheers and yelling, "Frogman Luck! Frogman Luck!"

It was a SEALs thing and everyone in the SEALs had hundreds of such stories of near misses and unexplained luck. "Frogman Luck has saved a lot of us from certain demise—on training, during missions and sometimes in the bars..." Chris remarked.

SAILBOAT

"Hey Mike! How's everything?" Chris called as he left the locker room and sprinted alongside another SEAL who lived at the marina. "Want to have a barbeque this weekend on the boats?"

"Sure thing!" Mike answered. Both young men were fit and energetic and looking forward to the rare weekend when they had downtime—a chance to relax. Their regular training schedule was grueling. And in addition to their training, Chris had just swam from his sailboat at a mooring off Fiddler Cove to shore with his clothing and gear wrapped up in a garbage bag to keep it dry.

After a few years in the SEALs, Chris had bought the sailboat, lived on it and swam daily from that mooring to his motorcycle on shore to get to work. Living in a boat at the mooring for six years was difficult while in San Diego, but it saved a ton of money and it made sense since he was deployed nearly eighty percent every year. A house or even a dock for his boat didn't make sense.

Some SEALs who thought the same way even lived in sea-land containers or VW vans in parking lots. For many, those were the days, living on the cheap, drinking and eating at Danny's or the Night and Day Café, and deploying overseas more than half the year—every year. It was a very demanding lifestyle but it made the relaxation and down times that much more cherished.

For Chris living on the boat was very Jimmy Buffet; single-handedly sailing his forty-eight foot ketch up the harbor to a restaurant that had docks to eat dinner and then sailing back. Chris usually docked at Peohe's in Coronado but only to cross the street to eat at Kentucky Fried Chicken or Pizza Hut.

For Chris an additional perk of this physically demanding lifestyle was that it kept him too occupied to think about being female on the inside. Too busy as a male, training and then having rare moments to kick back with the guys, he just kept the inner female pushed down inside, suppressed—at least most of the time.

The boat, however, was much nicer than a car or a box and was a good place for Chris because it was extremely isolated from nosey neighbors and provided a private place where when the longings became too intense Chris could sometimes allow his inner female out. He knew could not afford to be "outed" for cross-dressing in the SEALs so he had kept no female clothing while living on base, but at twenty-three, Chris needed a safe place to acknowledge his inner femininity and the boat provided that.

***

One Friday night after ten p.m. Chris was sitting on his boat dressed up in a black dress with a blonde wig, drinking. Mike's sailboat was moored about one hundred yards away from his boat and as he sipped his drink Chris saw Mike pull up to his boat and board. Soon Mike was also out on his deck with a drink—most likely a beer.

The hell with hiding! Chris thought and on sudden impulse and with a strong feeling of trust he stood, gathered a couple of beers and climbed into his row boat and rowed over to Mike's boat.

"Okay to board?" Chris asked with a smile on his face as he pulled up alongside holding up the beers. "Can I join you for a drink?"

"Hey, Chris!" Mike answered. "How's it going? Nice dress!" Mike added answering, "Yeah, no problem, come aboard."

Chris boarded and together the two SEAL brothers sat on the deck drinking and talking.

Mike asked how things were and Chris answered, "Fine," explaining with a chagrined smile, "I dress up once in a while to relax."

"Cool," Mike answered sipping his beer. "You don't look too bad," he added with a genuine smile. And then in an after thought—perhaps worried that Chris had more in mind, he commented, "I have a girlfriend and I'm happy with her."

"Yeah, she's a cool girl," Chris nodded. "I only do this once in a while," he explained. "I'm not gay or trying to get others to do this! It just makes me feel good to dress up sometimes…"

"It's cool," Mike said laughing as they sipped their beers looking out at the starry night over the balmy sea. Then with caution creeping into his voice Mike warned, "But be careful, Chris. Many of the team guys wouldn't take well to your dressing like that."

The drinking continued late into the night when the beers ran out at which time Chris got up to leave, stepped over the boat's side intending to get back in his rowboat but instead fell overboard.

Both men laughed as a drunkenly, Chris climbed back into the small boat and rowed back to his sailboat for the night. That night Chris slept with a heart filled for once with the acceptance and positive regard of knowing someone else had seen his true self and been cool with it.

VICTORIA'S SECRET—
SOMETHING FOR MY SPECIAL LADY

After a few more years of trainings and deployments and more suppression while on the road, Chris was home and once again, the longing to contact his "inner girl" was overwhelming. The urge had resurged in full force. Perhaps it was all the threats—having made it through the deployments and making it back safe, because for him dressing up had always been a comforting ritual, an escape from his father's violence. Now perhaps it had also become an escape from all that wasn't right in his life and his marriage—an attempt to right things by experiencing himself totally as a girl. The female gender identity was getting too much to suppress; Chris needed to see again the inner girl and experience her as he felt she really was. Just like before, he broke his vow and found himself at the mall.

"Are you looking for something for your special lady?" the sales girl asked as Chris walked into the Victoria's Secret store. It was a quiet time so there weren't many customers, but Chris felt dizzied looking at the array of bras: lacey, satin, smooth, red, blue, purple, pink and black and matching panties lining the walls, rolled up in neat drawers and placed artfully on circular tables. Everywhere there were headless flesh colored mannequins dressed in panties, garter belts and bras.

"Yes," Chris answered, smiling shyly as the girl drew him deeper into the store.

"What size is she?" the sales girl asked.

"I don't know," Chris hesitated, unsure how to reply. "Like my size," he suddenly answered.

"Do you know her *bra* size?" the girl asked, patiently smiling at his reference to himself.

"You mean how big she is?" Chris asked.

"Yes how close to *your size* is she?" the girl persisted.

"Kind of exactly," Chris answered, sheepishly gazing into the sales girl's eyes.

"Oh, I see," the girl said and suddenly smiled knowingly. "I can help you, no problem!" Then turning to the racks and taking a particularly alluring bra down she asked, "Do you like this one?"

"Yes!" Chris answered and together they picked out three bras, some silicon gel cups and a garter belt. Chris eagerly paid and exited the store.

Driving home with a package for their "special girl" from Victoria's Secret is undoubtedly an erotic experience for most men, Chris thought to himself. *They fantasize on their way home about giving their gift and saying to their special lady, "Go put it on and let's see how it looks" —and all that follows from there.*

It was the same for Chris except he was thinking about his own inner girl—himself. He only saw his "special lady" every few years when he allowed her to come out and "dress up". Tonight would be one of those nights.

Wedding Bells & Bosnia

After the first two years of buying and discarding female attire for his femme self, Chris suppressed himself entirely. He might look at women's clothes in the stores, but he didn't allow himself to buy anymore. After all he was a U.S. Navy SEAL.

Meanwhile, there was no shortage of girls for the SEAL teams and everyone was pairing off. Chris found himself dating Shelly just because she was there—he didn't feel much choice because at the time he didn't ever envision the freedom to come out as a transgender person, much less transition his body into that of a woman. Shelly was nice and he ended up pursuing her even though he knew it wouldn't work; he wanted to be the woman in the relationship as always—or just be alone, which was better in his mind. They dated a few times before he deployed to the Far East. They wrote back and forth, and upon his return from deployment with the pressure to be "normal," he set up a hiking trip for the two of them in Yosemite Park. There they camped on Half Dome and hiked around the park, getting intimate as well.

Afterward, Chris prepared to go to Bosnia for another deployment, a fast turn-around—which he preferred as working in the SEALs kept Chris's mind and body completely preoccupied from his angst over being female. But then he got a stressed call from Shelly with the words, "I'm pregnant. "

They quickly met to discuss: Shelly could raise the child alone or he could be involved. Chris in his mind had to do the right thing—his upbringing and the church and all the other pressures only had one conclusion: "We'll get married." Chris hoped for the best, but knowing he would be gone a lot helped.

Shelly finally agreed but found it bewildering, as they barely knew each other and on top of that, Chris had to deploy to Bosnia two days after they wed.

"Don't worry," Chris said to her after they'd hurriedly set up their life together. "I've left you with a pack of twenty blank checks." He went on to explain how much money was in the account and basically handed over his life to her as he went off to fight. So their married life began. And

Chris left home thinking, *Maybe I won't return and she'll live happy with my military survivor benefits and the 250K life insurance.*

***

"I dress up sometimes," Chris admitted to Shelly a month after he returned from Bosnia. He desperately needed to make contact with his inner female, dress up and feel himself as a woman, but because there was no good place to do so amidst the grueling training and deployment schedule except in the safety and privacy of their home late at night, he needed to explain to Shelly.

"What do you mean, you dress up?" Shelly asked, horror filling her face.

"I like to wear panty hose and a dress sometimes," Chris answered in a matter-of-fact voice, trying not to give away any of his anxiety. "I like to dress up as a girl."

Shaking her head, Shelly walked away in consternation. She was pregnant; her husband was not likely to be around much; he was a good earner but could be killed at any moment—and now this? She didn't want to hear anymore.

Chris could never admit that he thought he was experiencing himself totally as a girl. *Wrap that up tight in a bottle, lock it and put that in a safe then cement it shut, DO NOTHING,* was Chris's inner vow. This was a man's world and being discovered as a transgender individual would never fly. So he tried to keep his "female" persona separate from Shelly and the SEALs—literally it did not and could not exist. Although he resumed self-comforting by dressing up late at night after the boys were in bed, he never explained to Shelly how much it truly meant to him to be able to wear women's clothing in an attempt to connect his exterior to how he felt in his soul.

MORE FROGMAN LUCK

Whereas things at home with Shelly were tense, when Chris went on his frequent out-of-town (and often out-of-country) trainings with the SEALs, life was simple. The focus was totally on the physically and mentally demanding tasks at hand and the pace didn't let up until everyone had reached and gone well beyond their limits of exhaustion. Then it was time to sit around and pound back beers or collapse into sleep, repeating the same daredevil tasks again the next day.

Chris functioned well with no time or energy to think about male or female—only a focused concentration on mastering whatever task was set in front of the team that day, whether it be fast-roping from a helicopter, climbing a mountain cliff, training in a jungle, boarding boats, high elevation sky diving, blowing things up or shooting.

It was a good family for Chris, a place where he knew he was needed and belonged. And the rules were simple: perform well, never fail, never let a brother down, keep going no matter what. At least in this "family" Chris could make the grade.

***

"I can't believe we burned down the beer hooch last night," Jim laughed.

The guys had just spent four weeks training and running around the desert in Niland, California—a place many referred to as the armpit of California because the only cool thing was "Jesus Rock." The night before the guys had been blowing off steam, boozing late into the night and when their bonfire needed more wood, they had—under the influence of too much alcohol—decided to tear apart their beer hooch, throwing the plywood into the fire and when they needed more, they tore up the benches as well and fed them into the fire.

"It's our day off—what should we do?" Sammy asked as the guys were lying around after breakfast.

"What do you think of water-skiing on the canal?" Kyle asked, referring to the huge irrigation canals running through it that carried water from the Colorado River to the farm fields of California. "See that big piece of plywood left over. I think we could rig that up as a giant water ski." That got all the guys interested. Chris laughed, ready to have a rare moment of camaraderie that would just be fun—although with the SEALs even the fun often went to the next level of physicality given they were all in top physical condition and trained in ingenuity.

Soon the guys had the sheet of plywood rigged up with one-inch tubular nylon and a Humvee arranged on either side of the canal to drag it down the waterway.

"Who're the skiers? I think it will take two guys," Johnny offered.

"I'll take it," Sammy volunteered and Bill took the sideman position. The men both hitched their hands over the edge of the plank, and the Humvees on either side of the canal gunned their engines. Soon the plank holding both men was racing along the canal as the Humvees on either side dragged them atop the plank through the water—waterskiing the SEAL way. As they gained speed, the plank suddenly started taking water down the front and it plunged to the bottom of the canal. Sammy and Bill still held on, as the board continued moving forward, although now way slower underwater. The nylon stretched as the Humvees kept going.

One of the guys in the Humvee yelled, "Stop! They're gone!!!!????"

"Fucking awesome! They are diving it to the bottom," another answered as most of the guys cracked up laughing.

Bill floated to the surface fifty yards back. Sammy still clung on underwater. The plywood was moving very slow and the lines attached to the Humvees were pulled tight and still stretching. Confused, the drivers of the Humvees stopped.

The plank with Sam still attached suddenly launched out of the water upwards, taking flight. Sammy held on at high speeds through the air for about half a football field before letting go and miraculously splashing back down into the canal, while the plank flew past the now-stopped Humvees and crashed into the side of the canal.

"Fucking Frogmen!" Kyle screamed, laughing. Everyone ran to the place where Sammy had landed. They were all laughing—no one was hurt, nobody was dead.

After a moment of stunned silence, the rest of the team started yelling, "Frogman Luck!" Broken only by the voice of the Chief saying, "Clean this up before the Officers find out, and destroy that video tape."[7]

DOG & PONY SHOWS

It was the Fourth of July, 1996, and Chris was in a helo at 1000 feet above the San Diego Harbor, heading for Boy Scout Landing. This was the famous Fourth of July SEAL team demonstration—showing off all of the capabilities of the water warriors. As the helo flew over Coronado, Chris leaned out to look around. There were sailboats and yachts everywhere, girls in bikinis and lots of drinking going on. The helo zoomed in closer and Chris saw the crowds cheering and waving American flags. Shelly, with the baby in her arms, was one of hundreds on the beach waving. Looking down at her Chris thought, *She deserves better* and wished he could be the "normal" husband she needed but never would be. *It's a good thing we keep so busy,* Chris thought about how he was rarely home, knowing the constant trainings and deployments allowed their marriage to survive.

A group of SEALs—Chris included—were in swim gear getting ready to do a low pass, limp duck insert. The helo passed back in front of Boy Scout Pier, ten feet by ten knots.

"Push the boat out!" Jason, their team leader, yelled. "Go! Go! Go!" The guys pushed the boat out and jumped out after it. For a moment everyone was suspended over the water. Then the SEALs cut the lines from the platform, started the motor and got the boat going as it landed in the water and headed for the beach. The crowd went nuts.

"I hate dog and ponies," Kyle complained later adding, "This sucks. How about a war or something?"

"Civilians hooping it up for something we do everyday; gotta love this job!" Chris answered as he drained his beer glass.

Six years later as similar crowds watched in shock and awe as the New York City Twin Towers got plowed into first, by one jetliner, than again by a second, the war dogs got their wish—the wish they now regret. Following 9-11 the "War on Terrorism" immediately ramped up and for the SEAL teams—and the entire military for that matter—it didn't let up for the next decade and more. And while Chris could have easily bailed out of the SEALs at that point, he stayed in, taking on some of the hardest foes our country would ever face.

Lost UAVs & Tank Battles

The SEALs trained hard and were deployed often, but the entire game changed after 9/11. Immediately the tempo increased and the SEALs were quickly shipping off, first to Afghanistan and later to Iraq. With training, which often took place out of state and out of country, and the combat deployments, Chris was rarely home. When he was gone, Shelly ran their home and raised the boys. Chris welcomed the frequent deployments; it was a relief to the pressure of being a husband—a role he didn't feel capable to fulfill. Deploying and training with the SEALs was something Chris was good at, and it felt good to be needed at such an important job, but mostly he couldn't wait to get away from the continued self doubt and wishes to live as a female that overtook him every time he went home, about two to three months a year.

When he was home Chris was moody and agitated, unable to be his real self with Shelly and unable to make good contact with his sons, the second of which had now been born. With no way to be his authentic female self and not able to love even himself, he was at a loss for how to love them either. It was better to just avoid it all, better to be deployed than home where he couldn't be himself, and to risk being killed—because at least in that event his sons would receive his life insurance and Chris's problems would be over.

So after 9-11 Chris signed up for every deployment he could go on. And there were plenty to go on.

It was April, 2003 and Chris and his SEAL team were crossing into Iraq, part of the many Special Operations troops well inside Iraq before President Bush and the military initiated Shock and Awe, their grand ground and air assault.

Following the tradition of the precursors of the SEALs—the Underwater Demolition Teams (UDT) from World War II, who had also preceded the Marines landing—Chris and his mates took every opportunity they found to leave handwritten messages to their Marine Corps brothers that read: 'USMC, Welcome to Iraq'. The messages were in homage to the notes of their WWII predecessors.

Some weeks later, Chris was involved in the battle for Basrah, the biggest tank battle since World War II. Together alongside the British Royal Marines and the commandos, the SEALs had the responsibility to secure the Shatt al-Arab (S.A.A.) and take Saddam's Basrah Palace, a fortress along the river that was heavily guarded by Saddam's Republican Guards.

"We need to get 'eyes on' before we move in," the British Commander outlined the plan. He explained that Chris, along with his SEAL team, would be taken up river by the Special Warfare Combatant-craft Crewmen (SWCCs), or the crewmen that ran the boats, in a Special Operations Craft-Riverine (SOC-R) armored boat. They'd move up the river getting as close as close as possible to the palace—hopefully without being detected by the Republican Guards.

"Fly your UAV and get some ground truth," the Commander said, turning to Chris. Once the men were inserted along the river into Saddam's backyard, Chris was to launch and pilot his hand-held, five-foot wingspan unmanned aerial vehicle (UAV), the Pointer, which could fly silently and go undetected overhead and perform the aerial reconnaissance. That way the British and American troops would know what to expect in the coming days when they assaulted Saddam's Basrah Palace.

Republican Guards are his top dogs—top of the bad guys! Chris thought to himself as he boarded the heavily armored and gunned up SOC-R and took his place alongside the SWCCs. *These guys are war heroes driving these boats everyday on this river. Thanks to them we get to sneak and peek! These guys never have a place to hide or duck out,* Chris thought watching them ready for the mission.

The SWCCs, along with the SEALs, were nearly all entirely exposed to potential gunfire in the SOC-R boats navigating like this on a narrow river mission. If they were detected by an enemy contingent crawling alongside the river's edge for instance and taken in a well-coordinated ambush they could potentially all be wiped-out. Thus the familiar five weapon mounts were all manned for a full three hundred sixty degree offense or defense as the case might be. These were tanks on the water.

No one knows we're here, Chris thought to himself as he felt the adrenalin surging. It was night when they set out from their dugout holes in the ground, a full moon overhead. The SOC-R boat was camouflaged and had just taken position close enough to the palace. Looking around him Chris smiled at seeing the guys all with green and black grease painted faces. *They'll never expect the Pointer!* Chris thought to himself, proud of how it operated in near silence.

Chris was newly certified as a UAV pilot. And although drones had been in the military toolkit for years now, the launch and remote piloting of these small UAVs was still new and largely untested in battlefield conditions. The Predator drone had cut its teeth in the Balkans but the use of hand launched mini-drones like the Pointer (and later the Raven) was still a new procedure in combat.

In many ways Chris felt like a test pilot; he had flown and crashed so many drones over the years perfecting the UAV and perfecting the tactics involved—just like the original test pilots. But this time would be a first for him—Chris had not yet launched a hand-held drone from one of the SOC-R boats.

"Getting close," the crew signaled and as he'd been trained, Chris stood up with the readied UAV in his hand and threw it hard into the air to launch it into flight but somehow something went wrong. It caught for about forty yards, fluttered and then took a downward dive instead.

"Fuck!" Chris swore under his breath as he saw the UAV take off for a bit and then head downward rather than up into the night sky. "Fuck!" he swore again—still under his breath—as he watched it hit the water and crash.

It was what the SEALs call a hero to zero moment.

Shoot me now! Chris thought to himself. *Just kill me! Right here right now!* His sense of mortification was so strong that as he immediately leaned over the boat's edge and fished the UAV out of the water, he wished he could drown himself. The other back-up UAV was out of commission from other missions and needed repair. There were no other UAVs.

The mission totally and utterly failed in that one moment—whether it was his failure to throw it properly, a malfunction or something else, no one could know. The SWCCs waited for Chris to repack the gear and then turned around heading back to their encampment—the holes in the ground where the TEAMs were hiding out—where he had to face everyone.

They all know I fucked up! Chris thought to himself as he wished to fade into nonexistence. *Couldn't some sink hole open up and swallow me now!* Chris wished. *I one hundred percent failed it!*

In the next days the British and U.S. teams would carry out the mission and although they succeeded in taking down Saddam's Basra Palace, Chris would never completely get over his sense of failure and overwhelming guilt. He would often think to himself of that moment, replaying it like a traumatic memory over and over again in his mind. He'd ask himself, *How many lives could have been saved? Could we have done better on the assault? How many souls on both sides would still be walking this earth if I hadn't fucked up?*

Chris accomplished many other successful UAV missions in that war, and his citation for a Navy Commendation Medal with "V" from this time period reads:

To Chief Quartermaster (Sea, Air and Land) Christopher Beck, United States Navy

For Heroic achievement in connection with combat operations against the enemy while serving as Liaison Naval Officer assigned to SEAL Team Five in support of Operation Iraqi Freedom from April to June 2003. As unmanned aerial vehicle pilot, Chief Beck provided special reconnaissance and force protection for Special Boat Unit Two on riverine patrols into enemy held territory. He also conducted more than 18 high-risk combat missions into Baghdad, Iraq resulting in the capture of six senior ranking members of the former Iraqi regime. Chief Beck's courageous actions, personal initiative, and loyal dedication to duty reflected great credit upon him and were in keeping with the highest traditions of the United States Naval service.

Still, he would carry this failure with him forever. He would see others make mishaps and his depth of forgiveness was extreme, of course after he chewed them out for the screw up when necessary. Empathy for everyone, the hero and the zero, was what Chris carried inside—although when it came to himself, he was still very demanding and continually suppressing and denying the inner female.

The Sheepdog & the Reindeer Games

"Hey baby, nice ass!" Robbie shouted out the window and Jason started whistling. The guys were glad to be back and they were pumped. It was summer time and Chris lived and worked in Virginia Beach now, where the girls were dressed in bikini tops and cut off shorts.

"Stop it!" Chris said to them. "Don't do that, it's not cool"

"What's the problem man?" Robbie asked. "They were hot!"

"Girls don't like to be treated like that!" Chris answered, boiling under the collar. Inside he could feel his "inner girl" rising in anger but he didn't know how to explain that. "It's disrespectful! Degrades them," he added feeling a bit lost, like many women do when they don't know how to explain to men that they don't appreciate their sexually harassing comments.

Chris remained the "sheepdog" defending and watching over those that couldn't or weren't able to defend for themselves. He was a vigilante of the oppressed and fought prejudice and bullies. He felt himself both oppressed and bullied but was able to fight and win on behalf of others, most of the time.

***

The deployments to Iraq and then Afghanistan were coming fast, with few breaks in between and the guys needed to blow off steam. As the Teams went off for weeks at a time for trainings, it was inevitable that while on the road someone would eventually suggest going to a strip club.

It was a group thing so Chris went along, trying to fit in. As the girls gyrated and spun around the shiny silver pole, slowly rising up and down it while stripping off pieces of clothing, Chris felt mortified watching and kept asking them in his mind, *Why do you do this? Go back to school!* Meanwhile his SEAL buddies, Jonnie and Shredder were having a great time.

"God! Look at her tits!" Jonnie gawked and yelled out.

"Look at that ass!" Shredder screamed.

Why are they like that? Chris thought, looking around at the men he worked with—and loved as brothers. *I just don't get it! Why do they get such a kick out of these ladies doing this? It's like a live porno magazine.*

I like looking at girls—even in Playboy—to appreciate how beautiful they are and how I wish my body looked...but I don't get it. These women make good money, but it's a shame—they could do so much more. Chris sheepishly handed over a $10 bill to the girl serving drinks while saying a shy "Thank you!"

THERE'S A WAR ON, BUT NO ONE SEEMS TO KNOW

By the time his two boys, Max and Henry, were five and seven-years-old, the "War on Terror" was in full swing. Chris had become a battle-hardened warrior and for the most part had totally pushed down the "inner girl". He knew his country needed him—as a man and a warrior—and he was doing his duty.

But between the traumatic bereavement of losing too many loved ones—brothers on the battlefield who he had made his true family—and the constant disowning of his female gendered self, Chris was constantly angry. On the battlefield anger was useful. But when he was home—which was rarely, it wasn't.

Bearded and riding in on a motorcycle after a full day of training, often with his drinking buddies accompanying him, Chris saw that his two sons had no interest in knowing him. He was a stranger that punched holes in the wall when he got angry and that fought with their mom. For the most part Max and Henry hid behind their mother's skirts rather than try to reach out to this bearded, angry stranger who was their father.

You don't even know me, do you? Chris would think to himself when they shrank away from him. But with his PTSD and self-denial, Chris was too emotionally overwhelmed to reach out to his sons to create a safe harbor for them to approach.

Most nights in fact—if he came home alone without his buddies, Chris became obsessive. He would stand in front of the mirror and practice speed draws, pulling his pistol from its holster and practice firing it. He'd do this for hours, completely consumed with the need to train, train, and train some more. In the end it paid off: he got on the record boards shooting the six-plate test at Shaw shooting school—barely over half a second hitting six head plates from the holster draw. Of course this skill was useful on the battlefield, but it did nothing to endear him to his family.

Shelly saw a stranger as well. And worst of all in her mind was that Chris sometimes dressed up like a woman when they went to bed.

"That's disgusting!" she'd tell him completely mystified as to why a man would want to wear women's clothing. "Don't ever do that in front of the boys." She worried he would mess them up somehow. Neither Chris nor Shelly talked about anything more than bills or current needs. Chris was isolated and confused and just didn't know how to express it. He understood Shelly's perspective and was angered that he had to do this. He wished he could just be normal and was so envious of everyone else and their "normal."

But he knew if he couldn't be normal, then maybe it was better he was out fighting terrorists—staying away in isolation would save them from him and his demons.

So, Chris just kept plodding along living in a foggy dream world, wishing he was dead or transported out of this life and could start over. Work did provide a release from the self-loathing and dark thoughts he experienced whenever he slowed down. When he was with the Teams he was useful, doing something positive and he gave everything to it—one thousand percent. But always upon return, the angriness arose.

In reality, Chris was fighting on two fronts: one in which his SEAL team brothers were being maimed and killed in battle in events that were highly traumatic; the other an inner struggle for which he also had no easy answers. He could maintain a strong façade when he was busy war fighting but when he came home and was again faced with his impossible transgender situation for which he had no hope of a good resolution, he felt edgy and depressed.

Back from his eighth deployment, it was a breezy night in San Diego when Chris headed over to Imperial Beach to meet up with Paul, a motorcycle buddy who he had met two years previously when they witnessed a guy in their neighborhood beating up his girlfriend and separately ran to the scene.

"I'm back, alive and I want to get shit-faced," Chris had told Paul over the phone when they arranged to meet.

"Nice disguise," Paul said when they met, shaking hands and hugging briefly. Chris still had his full beard and longish dark hair—part of the uniform he wore to pass among the locals.

Chris thought this was funny; he was a woman disguised as a SEAL who grew a beard to disguise himself as a Pashtun. He was probably the only woman that ever sat at the head of a meal with Mujahideen Commanders at a shura.

The two buddies had been seated at the Filipino bar since four p.m. and now at eleven the bar was full of good looking girls in short skirts and high heels and little halter tops. Most of the good-looking girls were gravitating toward the guys in khakis and button down shirts—the ones with money—and ignoring Paul and Chris.

"Look at all these people—so aimlessly happy!" Chris said as he gazed glassy-eyed down the bar. Paul nodded.

"They don't even know there's a fucking war going on," Chris said as he picked up another shot and threw it back. "We are over there fighting and dying in the muck and blood and they don't even know! They're making shit loads of money, get all the girls and laughing and we make no money and we die for them. We just get shit on and nobody gives a crap about us! This is FUBAR!"

"Chill, buddy. You're alive!" Paul answered, lining up the shots again.

"HOOYAH!" Chris yelled smiling, even though life felt more like a curse than a blessing. Picking up his shot, he smashed his glass against Paul's yelling, "I'm back from fucking Iraq and I'm alive!" the two slammed back their drinks and laughing together, put them down on the bar for refills.

"Are you two from the military?" a guy down the bar spoke up adding, "That war is so fucked up—we shouldn't even be in Iraq!"

"What the fuck do you know?" Chris said turning to him, his eyes blurry from drinking.

"You heard me. The military is just some big fucking war machine. America invaded and started the whole thing," the guy repeated.

Chris retorted, "You didn't see the torture chambers down in the basement of Uday's palace. Or the human bones strewn around a lions cage. You didn't hear the women and children screaming hysterically for their lives at the sight of any man in uniform—we didn't understand what they were saying, later translated to 'Don't rape me! Don't kill me!' These women and girls were picked up by old Iraqi military henchmen on a regular basis for 'games' then killed and left in the desert! If anyone else in the family, like a father, resisted they were all shot on the spot!" Chris ranted, "You don't know about the Kurdish city that was gassed, wiped out, as a lesson not to resist Saddam's rule!"

The guy stupidly continued, "Well they never proved it! And I didn't see any of that on the news. It's probably all made up and lies. Bush is the worst President of all time. The military should be shut down and give the money to the poor!"

Chris and Paul were both drunk, too drunk to be listening to anymore of this shit, and Chris was still feeling like he was on high alert—watching constantly for the shot that was going to take out one of his buddies. *We lost guys over there—shot for scumbags back home like this nutter!* he thought. And listening to this shit Chris suddenly found he had no patience for it—none whatsoever. Boom! Chris's fist found the guys jaw, and before the jerk could block the next blow, Chris rained down another four or five punches.

"Don't you ever fucking talk shit about warriors who defend freedom and liberty!" Chris shouted at him as a pack of guys pulled him back from beating the guy. "Our guys died for you to be sitting here tonight! Died for you to be an asshole? How about thanks at least and keep your bile to yourself," Chris shouted as Paul joined in the fight.

It didn't last long. The guy was down and bloody. Someone called the cops and two policemen were soon inside the bar throwing Chris and Paul up against the wall, cuffing them.

The evening had suddenly spun out of control. Instead of celebrating, Chris found himself drunk and messed up and hauled out of the bar—not as a war hero, but as a drunk criminal who couldn't hold his temper.

"These are *our* benches!" Chris, claiming territory for his side and to put distance between them and everyone else, was reverting to his warrior behaviors as they were pushed into a cell full of the dregs at the San Diego jail.

Seeing that these two were buddies, super drunk and super angry, everyone else backed off of the two benches to go sit as far as possible on the other side of the cell. Chris briefly noted that there was a junkie in the corner puking in the toilet and a homeless guy pissing himself in the corner. The rest of the degenerates had taken seats along the floor. Taking their places on the benches, he and Paul collapsed, laughing, and laid down, to sleep it off, with one eye open and watching out for everyone else.

Chris and Paul were released with no pending charges due to some screw up in paperwork, but Chris left the San Diego jail feeling shame, hurt and anger burning in his soul. *Doesn't anyone back home get it—how much we give for them to be free?* Chris asked himself as they were released and catching a cab back to Imperial Beach. *Could I just get some basic respect for that?*

After the night in jail and return home, Shelly added to the pain saying, "I want to take the boys and go stay with my mother for a little while."

"Good! Go," Chris answered sullenly. "Get away, go! You don't love me; the kids are scared of me and hide behind you even when I walk in the room. They don't even know me. I'm going back to Afghanistan any-way—it's the only place for me now. Go to your parents' house, just go."

That night he watched out the window as Shelly drove away with the boys in their car. He pulled out a bottle of booze, downed a few chugs and then went over to his cabinet and pulled out his pistol. Chris lay it on the coffee table, unsure what he wanted with it and then drank a few more mouthfuls. The thought of blowing his brains out crossed his mind—more than crossed his mind—but then he went, laid on the couch and flipped on the television instead.

Not tonight, not yet, he thought to himself. *Not tonight. Better to take the lead pill over there, give the kids some college...*

A Bad Turn in Afghanistan

This time it was Afghanistan. Chris had switched teams again to get redeployed quickly. The sun was shining brightly, an hour after morning call to prayer, as Chris maneuvered his tan Toyota car through the buzz of business and optimism in the bazaar. They were on their daily reconnaissance mission, and Chris was dressed as an Afghan—sporting a rough untrimmed dark beard that framed his face and hung down over his neck and buttoned up cream-colored cotton thobe. His hair was also roughly cut like the Afghans, and he had a wool Pashtun cap perched atop his head.

"My name means embers," Angar, the interpreter, explained as he leaned back talking to Ben the Army Ranger in the back. Ben had their assault rifle hidden under the blankets on the seat for now. Angar, dark skinned and smiling, was similarly dressed, also with a Pashtun cap and a long cotton thobe. Ben and Angar were getting into it about Pashto traditions and Chris was momentarily distracted.

"Shit! We went to far!" Chris announced adding, as they drove through a market. "This is protected area; we can't be here!" Chris searched his memory as he drove on, trying to pull up the map he'd memorized of the area. Soon they would be on dangerous turf.

A freshly-skinned goat carcass swung from a hook attracting flies. The smell of fresh kill combined with the scents of unusual savory herbs, filling the air to near sensory overload. Cars honked and motorcycles whizzed by. *As long as they don't slow down or stop near us,* Chris reflected silently remembering how the motorcycles in Iraq particularly carried IEDs. With that thought he took another turn, this time away from the bazaar, but still not in the direction he wished.

Always vigilant, Chris noted the solar panels standing along some of the rooftops, electric cables linking them to many of the nearby shops. Up ahead a pack of dirty goats was blocking the road, *better to turn again rather than get blocked in,* Chris reflected and took another right hand turn down yet another unknown Afghan street.

Suddenly six guys stepped out into the street, two more coming behind them—all toting AK 47's. Chris did a quick mental calculation: *8 AKs, I have a pistol. Ben has an M-4. We're dead!*

"Angar, talk to them! Make something up," Chris instructed in a low hiss. Angar started talking in the familiar dialect. At this point twelve more stepped out from the alleyways—twenty gunmen surrounding them on all sides.

Speaking Pashto, Angar explained that he was doing business in the area but they were lost. He pointed out Chris as his driver and Ben as a peasant worker. Chris and Ben dressed as locals can pass—and as peasant labor they aren't expected to talk when the businessman or leader is handling things. They stayed silent watching. In the back Ben was ready for the shit to hit the fan.

The gunmen came up to the truck and started looking in the front windows.

We are definitely dead now! Chris thought as his mind raced, trying to think ahead. His pistol was hidden from view, there was nothing to identify any of them in the car except the blood chit—the indestructible paper that both Chris and Ben carried in their clothing, hidden inside inner pockets, on which is written in six different languages a message that may save them if they get in serious trouble. It reads: "I'm an American. If you help me get to safety, you will be richly rewarded."

As if reading Chris's mind, the leader of the Afghans suddenly shouted gruffly pointing with his AK 47 to Chris in the truck: "American?"

Chris and Ben understood this word. Angar blanched. Something in the truck—maybe Chris or Ben—had not passed muster. They are discovered.

Making a calculated risk, Chris quickly reached deep into his pocket and pulled out his blood chit, showing just the American flag from it. He slowly showed it to the leader.

"Yes, we are Americans," he admitted, taking over the conversation, as Ben kept his finger on the trigger of the big gun.

I can take one or two of them out, maybe three, Ben thought to himself as he waited to see how Chris's admission was going down.

"We're going to the base on official business. Can you help us?" Chris asked.

Angar translated. The Afghans conferred and then one by one they lowered their guns.

They are friendlies! Chris, Ben and Angar thought in relief. The leader then told Angar which streets to take to get safely back to the base, avoiding the turf where they will likely be killed.

"I was so fucking ready to shoot!" Ben said as Chris pulled the truck away. "It was so close!"

"We were dead—totally outnumbered," Chris answered soberly.

"Yeah but I would have gotten two or three of them, maybe more!" Ben argued.

Angar and Chris remained silent, just happy to see the streets become recognizable again as they emerge back out of the Afghan maze of roads. *The base is close now,* Chris thought to himself.

I have to memorize that map again and again! Did a roadblock get set up? Did they move something or tear a building down? What the fuck? Chris thought as he headed back, berating himself for the wrong turn. He was in a tailspin and so hard on himself for *any* mistake, even though Chris had conducted over two hundred clandestine missions in support of his SEAL Team brothers and a Bronze Star Medal citation from this time period heralded him:

For heroic achievement in connection with combat operations against the enemy as a Military Source Operations Specialist for the Joint Task Force in support of Operation Enduring Freedom from April to September 2008. During this period, Senior Chief Petty Officer Beck conducted military source operations regarding insurgent activities with no loss of equipment or personnel. He distinguished himself on multiple raids by his leadership and personal combat actions, which directly resulted in the capture or elimination of numerous enemy combatants. Senior Chief Petty Officer Beck's distinctive contributions, unrelenting perseverance, and steadfast devotion to duty reflected great credit upon him and were in keeping with the highest traditions of the United States Naval Service.

PERILS OF TRAINING

In the SEALs the training is so tough that men get killed not only on deployments facing enemy combatants but also at times in preparation for combat. When they are training for close-quarters battle the door charges are real—as is the ammo—and if an operator screws up somebody can get badly injured, even killed. SEALs have been hurt and killed in parachute training, fast roping, diving, high speed driving and all the other drills they are put through. The high physical demands of the job and daredevil tactics create a strong team ethic that upholds a very high standard—no one can fail because death—even in training can literally be the result.

And if it's humanly possible, the SEALs have probably tried it—from boarding a fast boat from the skids of a helicopter that is hovering over the seas to swimming for hours on end to get to a desolate beach to dig in and sleep for the day only to move out that night to the target. Climbing mountains, crossing glaciers, parachuting from 30,000 feet, jumping across buildings, using magnets to climb skyscrapers–high speed, low drag, they can do anything to get it done. Achieving super human feats confers both a sense of awe and pride once they realize that they have met the standard, although these feelings are also coupled with a deep humility because the challenges and demands from the SEALs team trainers just keep on coming.

For Chris this constant demand to be a top performer—rising to and even exceeding the standards of professional athletes and to remain a top-notch highly and constantly trained warrior always ready to deploy at a moment's notice—allowed him to also stay inside of a constant tunnel vision of focus on the SEALs.

***

Back from Afghanistan and on training out at sea, Chris and the Team was doing ship boarding training. Shelly as usual was back at home with the boys—and Chris was away from home—out with the Teams. It was afternoon and they had two Rigid Hull Inflatable Boats (RHIBs) and from their drop-off point, they had an hour ride to meet an oil tanker out in the middle of the ocean. Their job was to sneak up on the tanker, hook up a ladder from their RHIB to the safety lines on the aft of the ship and climb aboard and "take over."

SEALs board ships in many ways and they practice this skill often as one of their primary missions. They do it from RHIBs, fast rope from helos or just jump from the skids of a helo right onto the deck of the ship.

"Many ways to board, many ways to miss-step and be killed doing it. Keep practicing and get good." Chris jokes.

The challenge in boarding from the RHIBs is that both boats are moving at once often going ten to fifteen knots in eight to ten foot seas and they climb up a thin wire "caving ladder" with only six inch rungs while loaded with about eighty pounds of gear, explosives and weapons.

In this training, Chris was the lead climber—the first guy up. He went up slick to the tanker's side and tied in the safety line to keep the grappling hook and ladder anchored to the ship.

As Chris climbed the wire ladder, ten-foot seas blasted the RHIB against the ship. Suddenly, the ladder snapped around and spun but held. The RHIB got hit again by a big wave and the ladder went very loose then suddenly snapped, sending Chris flying off into space. Chris landed on the center console of the RHIB, cracking his body armor back ceramic plate. Stunned and in pain, Chris lay on the floorboards of the RHIB near the .50 gunner near the front. His teammate Smitty began the climb to get the safety strap hooked so they could finish the mission—there was no stopping the SEALs.

Then 'Circus', a SEAL whose father owned the animals for a major circus and who had grown up with the carnies, kicked Chris who was still lying on his back in the RHIB saying, "Get up you lazy bum. We have to board this thing!"

Trained to never give in—no matter what—Chris got up, staggering at first, reached for the ladder and started the climb. Adrenaline or hard-headedness kept him going. Hours later when the ship was totally secure, its captain amazed that he had been "boarded" and the SEALs satisfied with their success, they were able to return to the base. There, Chris and the team cleaned all the gear and crashed out, tired from the long day.

The next day Chris was not moving so well. He went to the Doc and mentioned back pain, "right about here."

"Did you sleep on it bad or have an old injury?" the Doc asked.

"No, good sleep and no old injuries—but I fell off the ship and broke my body armor the other day." Chris nonchalantly answered.

The Doc immediately laid Chris on a gurney, strapped his head down and ordered x-rays. Chris's lower back vertebrae had a few cracks, as well as some disc problems. He was given a back brace and Motrin and sent home. This injury along with many others sustained along the way in his twenty years of serving as a Navy SEAL would leave Chris with a lifelong struggle with pain and eventually culminate in Chris's eighty percent disability rating at the end of his service career with.

Empathy Earned the Hard Way

In 2008, Chris was in Afghanistan again. His Team was sent into a village to catch a "bomb maker" who had already been "captured and released" and had evidently gone back to his old tricks.

Arriving at his compound late at night Chris and the SEALs surprised this Taliban in his sleep. But like most of them he slept with a gun near his bed. And like the rest, he grabbed his gun and tried to kill the SEALs as they entered but lost the fight.

The tough thing about such missions is that in nearly all of them the terrorists and insurgents do not live in barracks like regular enemy soldiers. Instead they live like regular people in homes and compounds surrounded by their family members, including their brothers, cousins and their wives and children. Some might argue that anyone living with a known terrorist shouldn't expect to be in safety, but that's a hard argument for wives and children who really don't have much choice in the matter.

In this case, the terrorist's wife and baby were in the same room and as the SEALs poured into the room shooting to match his opening volley, the man's wife began shrieking, crying and falling to the floor. Completely dependent on her man, her world had just been completely shattered. And her tiny baby was wailing in the crib nearby.

Seeing that the room was secure and that the others had moved on as more rooms had to be searched, Chris went to the crib and pulled the baby out. Kneeling down he helped the distraught wife stand up and handed the baby into her arms. Guiding her by her shoulders, Chris helped her make her way out into the courtyard area with some of the other women and children. His heart was filled with pity and sadness looking at the children and wives who had just lost fathers and husbands to a fight they would never win. At least in his case he knew his wife and sons would be cared for if he was killed, but these women and children had no such security net.

There was more shooting and searches while Chris stood guard over the women and children ensuring their safety from the firefights breaking out in various areas throughout the compound.

"We've got a VBIED!" Smitty yelled, indicating he had found a vehicle that was wired and full of explosives and ready for attack. As the SEALs readied to destroy the explosive laden vehicle, "Dawg" guided all of the women and children out of the compound onto a field up the road. Everyone else got ready to leave the area in the gun trucks (GMVs). But first "Rod" and Chris had the task to destroy the vehicle (VBIED) so it couldn't be used in a future attack.

Standing on a nearby rooftop Chris shot the car with a LAW rocket. It blew to pieces and fiery fragments from the explosion blew into the nearby building, lighting it on fire that then lit a few other buildings connected to it.

Fuck! Chris thought as his mind moved to the tearful women and children. Now their home was up in flames as well. Wishing he could do something to stop the conflagration, Chris knew there was not any choice but to exit. He and Rod loaded into their GMVs along with the other SEALs and everyone hit the road. As they drove away, Chris looked back and saw the women on the side of the road crying and holding their children, their houses burning in the distance. It would be a picture that would return again and again into his mind in years to come.

REENTRY

"You hate me," Shelly said to Chris late one night after he had just returned home from a deployment in Iraq.

"No, I don't hate you," Chris replied. "I don't love you like you want me to," he added alluding to the sexual shutdown between them.

She glared across the room, and he could see that it wasn't doing any good to talk. It never did, because Chris didn't say what needed to be said and also didn't give heed to her pleading silence.

Chris was exhausted. His nerves were frayed and his emotions were rough and ragged—he'd had "his head in the game" for so long, suppressing emotions and any feelings of vulnerability, and now to enter into his home where everything was "normal" and his wife and the boys were needy and emotional felt like getting hit with a tidal wave. And his clock was all turned around. It was hard to sleep at nights; he was used to going out and being on mission all night, not sleeping next to his wife.

If you want me to hate you, I'll hate you! Chris thought getting out of bed to go downstairs to watch the news and do quick draws with his pistol.

Work, training, drilling like this at home—he needed it. Anything obsessive that contributed to a positive sense of self worked to take his mind off of the pain and helped shut down his self-hatred, sense of failure and the near constant wish he had when he was at home to eat a lead pill.

Draw, shoot! Draw, shoot! Draw shoot! Chris practiced with his gun, shutting out the argument and all else as he repeated the motions, getting faster and faster with each hour he put in.

***

"What are you doing today?" Shelly asked the next morning as Chris sat silently staring blankly at the walls waiting for his coffee to cool down. "There are a few things I would like you to do."

"Geez Shelly! I just got home!" Chris answered, raising his voice.

"I don't understand," Shelly retorted, crossing her arms over her chest, tears welling up in her eyes.

"Oh fuck, Shelly!" Chris yelled and pushed back from the table going out to the garage to jump on his motorcycle and take off until midnight, anger and confusion eating away at him.

You're the best mother, Chris continued the argument in his head as he drove away. *But I'm getting driven away from you! I can't give you what you want—the family with the white picket fence. I'm not a man and I can't be your man. And beside that I have the SEALs to be loyal to. I love my friends! We fight together! We live and die together! I already buried twenty-six friends! I love my mission and the Teams! So I practice my profession! I'm a professional athlete times one hundred—we have the world as a ball field and go 24/7 for six months or longer. I practice and practice so that I'm a fucking guy! I'm an operator and been in the muck too long, and I have the Teams' six [their backs]!*

Little did he know that all she wanted was for him to take Max to the Boy Scouts that afternoon. Max was so proud of the work he had done in the Scouts and wanted to share this with his dad—just like all the other kids with their fathers.

One day Max would say to his mother, "I wish I had a different Dad."

If only Chris hadn't had such a bad temper. If only he had spoken to her instead of punching the wall. They walked on eggshells around him. It must have been torture for Shelly and the kids to be around Chris. It was torture for Chris to live isolated from them inside of his head and not have them at his side like a normal family but he had no idea how to fulfill his role as the man of the family when inside he felt himself to be a woman.

And he could never explain it to her—how hard it was over there, how many of the guys were gone. He did love and appreciate her—especially for being the good mother she was to their sons. But it was true: he couldn't love her the way she wanted to be loved. He wasn't the man and couldn't be the husband she needed.

Can someone please take care of me? Chris cried out inside his mind. *Can I be pretty? I'm always dirty! I'm always full of blood and muck! Can anyone take care of me?*

But these were all unacceptable things to be asking for. He wasn't supposed to want to be pretty—to want female things. He was the man of the house and responsible to take care of everyone else. And he was a SEAL—they were never supposed to feel vulnerable, bereaved, confused or overwhelmed. They were tough guys, the ones everyone else turns to for solutions. They were the problem solvers, never the problems. So there wasn't going to be anyone taking care of him, and his wife, not understanding any of this, began avoiding him also except to ask for a few things here and there. Their relationship was tense, full of confusion and sad rejection.

Divorce and coming out as a woman didn't even enter his mind at the time—coming out as a transgender individual just wasn't something acceptable in his world. It felt like announcing one was an alien from Mars. And to do so would have ended his career, his marriage, his friendships, his family of origin and basically everyone he looked up to, love and respected. So Chris did what he always did.

"Send me back over," Chris told his boss the next morning.

Chris was deployed with another team, and after saying goodbye to his sons who barely knew him and Shelly who seemed both relieved and worried to see him leaving, Chris thought to himself the same thoughts he had often enough: *Send me back over—maybe I'll get fucking whacked. That will give my kids $250,000. I'll be the behind the lines guy as much as possible.*

TALIBAN BIRTHDAY

It was June and the squadron Chris was currently serving on was set up in a military encampment near the border between Afghanistan and Pakistan. The Taliban had figured out how to set up 107mm Russian rockets on sawhorse-like structures that they used for aiming and launching their rockets from twenty to thirty miles away. It was impossible to retaliate because they cleverly used timers to delay the launch for their getaway and by the time the military located the rocket's launching point, the enemy would be long gone. .The camp was getting hit all the time randomly, but the worst was when it hit the town nearby. Not only did innocent Afghan people get hit, but the Taliban propaganda always blamed the Americans.

The SEAL team, as Standard Operating Procedures (SOP), kept Zulu hours. The other guys referred to them as the "Vampires"—waking in the early evenings to ready themselves to carry out their night missions and then returning in the early mornings—to sleep again during the days. By the time the sun was up but before the local muezzin's first call for prayers, the SEALs would be back at base if things went right. Upon their return the guys went to bed only after carefully reloading ammo, redoing food and water, readying their weapons, draping body armor over what looked like a suit stand, and only when all was ready to go again at a moments notice, did they then shower and head for bed.

In June, while the guys were sleeping in their barracks—all the gear carefully lined up, weapon, body armor, helmet and three-day backpack on stands next to each bunk, a building only twenty feet away exploded into shards.

"What the fuck was that?" Jamie, one of the SEALs, hollered jumping to his feet.

Cracking their door and peering out to gaze across the rock-strewn grounds, Otis answered, "Mortar again! Pretty far away, the wall next to FOB headquarters just took a hit!"

"Fuck that!" Jason said, and turning back to face the wall fell immediately back asleep.

Chris registered the conversation but barely woke up. He was used to it. The base came under mortar or rocket attack often enough and everyone was used to living in detachment mode, keeping their emotions at bay while in a conflict zone.

Indeed at this point in his career Chris had become so detached from fear—and also sometimes so willing to risk his own life to end the problems of having to face his gender identity issues—that he was often the one that would go roaring into the mountain caves shouting "Come out motherfucker" to the Taliban who might be hiding in there. Not many of the guys would do that, but Chris had learned to push his fear down deep while in the combat mode and he was also willing to risk his all in battle. So incoming mortar here on the base just wasn't a big deal when sleep was sorely needed.

Nothing we can do about it, might as well sleep! was the team's shared motto. They knew they'd be going out again tonight and that's when it mattered. *You want to be alert when you can make a difference. These rockets or mortars are just random and if your time is up, then it's up! Better to sleep now and put it out of mind.*

It was three p.m. when the guys woke for breakfast. June 21st, the summer solstice—today was Chris's birthday and the guys always made it special when someone had a birthday.

"Look's great, Cookie! Thanks man, we owe you for this one!" Spanky said, as he picked up the birthday cake he had arranged with the chow hall cook to bake for Chris. Spanky always had a way to make things happen and he was always in the right place at the right time.

"We've got steaks and they even gave us *twenty* lobsters for you buddy!" Jamie said as he stoked the grill up with charcoal, readying everything for their three a.m. supper. At ten p.m. the guys went to the chow hall for lunch and walking back to their barracks, incoming suddenly started hitting the area.

Boom! The explosion hit right next to Jamie. Matt, one of the OGA (Other Government Agencies) guys working with the team went flying into the air—a fragment or the rocket itself zippered across his back suddenly, cutting him in half. The others hit the ground, their hands over their heads. A hard fragment of metal screeched through the air and imbedded itself deep into Chris's arm.

***

"Happy birthday man! You got lucky, with just a small bit of metal from the Taliban for a present!" the old Vietnam encrusted doc said as he fixed up Chris's wound. Later, staring down at his bandaged arm Chris tried to push the vision of Matt out of his mind—severed across the shoulder blades by whatever had hit him.

I was right there beside him! Chris thought. *Damn! Take me, and let him get back to his family. Birthday or not, it could've and should've been me; I'm alone in this world, I don't need to be here for anyone!*

Don't Ask/Don't Tell—
Just Let me Lie Down & Die

In 2006, Chris and Shelly picked up right where they left off. Fed up, Shelly took the kids and moved to live near her parents in Minnesota.

As they left in the Volvo, Chris sat in his Chevy truck and drove beside them for a few miles. Max waved out the window with a smile on his face. Henry was in his car seat, waving both hands laughing. Crying, Chris almost crashed after he lost view of them and the car. They were headed off to a new life—a life without their father. Chris was devastated at the failure, confused and ready to give up.

He was alone now and had to try to build some semblance of a life. The only console he had now was to dive into his feminine side. Try to ease his soul and come to some kind of peace.

***

For years Chris had turned off his sexuality like a light switch and lived as a warrior, consumed with the battle—living basically asexual. For Chris the other SEALs were brothers and in the man's man warrior lifestyle, even if he had wanted to entertain sexual thoughts, there really was never any time to be thinking too much about sexuality. Blood, constant deployments, hard driving, fatigue and traumatic bereavement can all help shut down a sex drive. And until he resolved his body issues and got a girl body it would be too strange for him to engage in homosexual behavior that he didn't relate to.

But at some point Chris knew he would have to make peace with his body not matching his mind, not matching his soul. Psychologically Chris felt like a girl somewhere between eleven to sixteen. But since he had never allowed himself to express his female gender identity and because he was caught in a male body, Chris as a female still needed to go through adolescence—to learn how to be a girl and express her sexuality. Although that required dressing up and even moving into a female body. Now with Shelly gone, Chris tentatively explored that developmental stage. He sometimes went to the bars alone at night, dressed ambiguously—playing with an expression of his female self much like a teenage girl would—but most often he sat in the bars drinking and just feeling lost.

Chris also went to a few gay bars; they were filled with very nice people, open and caring. For the most part they understood what it was like to be different—what it was like to be hated and prejudice thrown at them. Chris saw himself growing close to the guys and the women that made up that scene. He was friends with all of them and none of them. And he played with the idea of going home with a guy, but it was too scary and also didn't fit his sense of self as a "straight girl".

Overt homosexuality was not tolerated in the military at the time—they were still running under a Don't Ask/Don't Tell policy—and Chris felt trepidation about crossing any borders—and he also didn't feel he was gay. But he also didn't feel he was a man, so he didn't really know how to negotiate a sexual relationship whilst in a man's body. He was lost—with no maps, no compass and no guides.

***

On one of his two-day leaves Chris went to Minnesota to visit his sons. Hoping to hang out, he waited for them to get home from school, but things didn't go as he hoped. His sons arrived home with friends in tow.

"You want to hang out now?" Chris had asked Max, his eldest.

"Dad, my friends are here!" Max had answered, embarrassment creeping into his voice.

"I'm only here for two days!" Chris said, taking Max off to the side and speaking in hushed tones.

"Friends are important!" Max argued, and perhaps deciding to let his early childhood hurt out he added, "Dad we learned this from you: friends are important—family doesn't matter."

Chris had walked out to his car—tears blinding his eyes—and drove off on a sudden "errand", thinking, *I messed them up so bad! I am worthless to them now, how can I go back and fix this? If ever?*

Later when he had returned to the house Shelley pointed out to him, "You showed up for *two days* and then you disappear again! What do you expect from them?"

It was true—he had no right to expect anything.

***

By the time he had carried out thirteen deployments, a couple hundred missions executing advanced tradecraft captures and served as the ground force commandeer in Afghanistan for all the missions he went on, Chris had seen a lot of death: death of the guys they took down, death of innocents, unfortunates that sometimes ran in the way of fire or were in a building that got hit, and death of his comrades. While many people have full-blown flashbacks of combat, Chris never allowed that into his mind: he was a master of detachment. He had trained himself too well to allow his PTSD to take over. Instead, he would see still snapshots of fallen friends and scenes. It was like still photos that appeared in his mind, one after the other. Chris tried to keep his feelings at bay, but it was upsetting and painful to vividly remember his fallen buddies. It was the worst at night. The live action would return in dreams and it would always be of those times when his buddies fell. And the question would always be the same, *Why did he die? Why him? He had a life. Why not me?* But like all SEALs Chris always pushed his PTSD down—never letting it get in his way or slow him down in accomplishing their missions. SEALs rarely admit pain, hardly if ever admit vulnerability—they are highly trained to just keep going and keep fighting, knowing and living by the credo that failure is not an option.

***

Chris was trained for night raids and vampire hours and as a result rarely slept well. He always woke around hit time—between two and three a.m.—and re-lived some aspect of what he'd been through. Likewise the pain from the many training and combat injuries he had sustained also often made sleep difficult to find. One night when he couldn't get to sleep, Chris had too much to drink and he was feeling alone and sad. Failure filled his mind and guilt over being alive when the others weren't.

Will I ever be able to be me? He asked himself as he pulled out some hard liquor and began to booze up. His pistol was on the shelf near the television and his eyes kept being drawn to it. *Take it and just get it done with now! You don't deserve to be alive,* a part of his mind said.

Another part watched the television. It was a show about kids in New Jersey getting drunk and being stupid. Chris flipped the channel and saw a show about the life of Michael Jackson with millions of fans around him screaming. *There's a real hero!* Chris thought sarcastically to himself. Then he changed the channel to basketball—more fans screaming, and then to football—more fans. Next he flipped to the "news" –it was showing Britney Spears and her latest drug relapse and her struggles with her two children. He changed the channel to some review of the Grammys with the "stars" going up on stage as they cried and told the audience how hard it was to get there and how wonderful life is. The "hero" on stage threw in some insult about the President and the war and how messed up America was, how we should be more like the French or more like Venezuela or some crap.

"What the fuck?" Chris asked himself and picked up his pistol. It was cold and he fiddled with the weapon, doing a press check, then laid the pistol back down on the table.

There's still so much out there to do, Chris thought, shutting off the TV and putting the gun down. *The easy way out is not the right way, especially when I still have my buddies over there in the sandbox—defending the rights of the heroes of the idiot box and our modern-day coliseums.*

WAR GAMES

Chris got a call one day from Bill Shepherd, a former Navy SEAL, NASA astronaut, commander of the International Space Station, and a recipient of the Congressional Space Medal of Honor. "We need your innovative experience and combat skill sets down here at SOCOM working for me," Shep, as he was known to his friends and colleagues, said into the phone.

"Yes, sir!" Chris answered, effectively leaving Naval SEALS Special Warfare Development Group (NSWDG)—one of the best commands in the Department of Defense. He moved to Tampa to work in the Office of Science and Technology at the U.S. Special Operations Command (SO-COM), the unified command for the worldwide use of Special Operations of the Army, Navy and Air Force.

Shep and Chris clicked immediately due to their intense science and technology (S&T) spirit and love for getting the best new gear to the guys in combat. Chris finally found the mentor he'd needed all his life. He distinguished himself by starting many new projects, with four standout innovations and inventions that are still being used in combat in Afghanistan and around the world to this day.

For once in his life Chris felt truly appreciated, although he was also tired of being constrained by the military rules from living as the woman he felt himself to be. He was also tired from many other things, in fact—all the battles, all the death he'd seen—and he was ready to retire and free himself. But Special Operations needed him, and Chris didn't feel like he could break away and retire or leave the fight. And that was all about guilt—his survivor guilt.

As Chris set up his new home in Tampa, he pulled an Ansel Adams print out of a box and looked at it for a few minutes before deciding where to hang it. The black and white print showed the moon over Half Dome. It had been a possession of Hound Dog, his deceased SEAL team brother. After he was killed, Hound Dog's mother had given the nicely framed picture to Chris. The loneliness of the picture was intensified knowing Hound Dog was no longer here. Chris took a nail and hung it in a prominent place in his living room—a reminder of all the ghosts that walk with him daily.

I have to stay in somehow. I feel like I owe, Chris thought as retirement approached. *I don't deserve to even be here! Chris thought to himself. I should have died a thousand times! My life is in shambles. They had families, they were good men; I wish I could trade places with them.*

These were the guilty thoughts that kept Chris serving his country, paying back for the deaths of those who didn't deserve to die. And instead of congratulating himself on the dozens of missions he had flown successfully when there had been calls for close air support, he emotionally beat himself up and stayed mired in shame and guilt for his few failures.

Meanwhile, even after thirteen deployments—seven into combat zones and many more than most SEALs have under their belt at retirement—Chris also kept paying against some unseen debt ledger that could never be satisfied because he was so confused about himself.

Survivor Guilt

While there was a war going on and the SEALs needed experienced warriors like him, Chris didn't feel like he could break totally away after retirement or leave the fight. And that was all about guilt—survivor guilt.

I don't deserve to even be here! Chris would think to himself. *I should have died a thousand times!* And then his mind would wander to the guys who did die—while he remained alive.

What about Marty? Taking a piss when he stepped on a mine—I was only half the SEAL he was! His mind would wander to the guys who died at Taliban checkpoints. *I shouldn't be here. Those guys should!*

Following 9-11, as the SEALs began going out on frequent deployments—first to Iraq and then to Afghanistan Chris thought often about Frogman Luck. Every SEAL had at least a dozen stories of Frogman Luck—and it was often considered epic that the SEALs were so lucky, maybe not luck, but it was thousands of hours of training—but then again, some weren't so lucky. Some didn't make it home.

I've been in room riddled with bullet holes, Chris often thought to himself, racked with guilt. *Sure most people [wrongly] aim high and we trained our asses off on how to avoid getting hit, but how did I get out? Frogman Luck? I can't believe Tom didn't make it back, that guy was tough as nails, top of the food chain.*

Hound Dog had been killed in Sacramento at the beginning of the war—nonsensically by a drug dealer in his hometown, total weird, bad timing.

And what about Chris Kyle? One of the greatest SEALs that ever lived—and he gets shot by some fucked up wannabe, a Marine who says he's got PTSD. It doesn't make sense!

Why did I survive? I should have never come back. I kept trying to go back to be there with my brothers! Why was I that lucky? I was in the kill zone a dozen times!

I can personally name twenty-three of my friends, my brothers who died in the war, Chris reflected to himself late at nights, early in the morning, throughout the day. *Over eighty SEALs have died since Iraq and Af-*

ghanistan started! We lost a lot of guys. And look how fucked up I am; my life is in shambles. They had families, they were good men; I wish I could trade places with them.

These were the guilty thoughts that Chris kept feeling and kept him serving his country, paying back for the deaths of those who didn't deserve to die. Chris also kept paying against some unseen debt ledger that could never be satisfied because he was also so confused about himself—he didn't feel that he deserved to live.

Too often his mind flashed back to battles where someone had died and thought about how if something had been different, it could have changed many outcomes. He'd replay his failed UAV launch in Iraq, when the UAV plunged into the river instead of taking flight. *It could have been the controller,* Chris would argue with the unseen accuser in his mind. I *started the aircraft but the engines weren't right,* he'd think to himself, wondering if the modifications later made to the aircraft were because it had failed or because he had failed.

Instead of congratulating himself on the dozens of missions he had flown successfully when there had been calls for close air support—flying hundreds of test aircraft and newly designed UAVs—he mentally flogged himself for failing once. Instead of giving himself credit for having served on the "learning edge" and given valuable feedback to the designers so the UAVs could function better and succeed more often, he emotionally beat himself up and stayed mired in shame and guilt for his few failures. Indeed Chris had built three new UAV systems and gave operational feedback from the battlefield. And he basically had served as a test pilot developing the entire systems that were now saving many military lives.

"I had a ton of successes and I crashed more than anyone else," Chris told Anne. "It was like being a test pilot. I was one of the UAV test pilots!" Indeed while serving at the Development Group Chris received awards for his UAV piloting and for perfecting many advanced weapons systems and tactics. Despite his citations and medals, Chris however was plagued with guilt and the guilt kept him going and volunteering for ever more difficult jobs. Chris felt he had to keep making up for everyone else; keep driving to the max, 100 miles an hour.

And now finally after twenty years, thirteen deployments with many into combat zones—many more than most SEALs have under their belt at retirement, Chris still doubted he'd given enough. He'd paid and repaid, but still he felt indebted and guilty for being alive. *I owe a debt to a bunch of ghosts!* He'd think to himself.

DRESSING FOR DINNER

At home in Tampa, Chris could spend his evenings alone dressed as a female, but at work he remained strictly presenting as a male. Now on a trip back to Virginia, Chris arrived for dinner at his mother's house in Maryland after a full day of working at the base. Chris's father wasn't there as he mostly stayed in their New York home—his parent weren't divorced but didn't spend all their time together anymore, finding their own peace in keeping their own homes.

"Hi Mom," Chris said as he came into the kitchen. Then uncorking a bottle of wine he poured himself a glass and sat next to her relaxing as she prepared their dinner. "I need to wash up," he said when his glass was emptied. "Can I get dressed up for dinner?" he added as he took his bag and headed for the guest room.

"Yes of course," Kate answered as she busied herself over their dinner. "Wear what you are comfortable in."

Chris disappeared into the guest room and wanting to dress as he did most nights in Tampa these days, he showered and then taking his girl clothes out of his tote bag put on a dress, hose and high heels topping it all off with a wig and make-up. Walking out of the guest room into the kitchen he waited for his mother's reaction. True to form she kept her emotions mostly hidden and under control.

"Wow, that is an interesting outfit!" Kate commented and continued laying out the table. Both sat down and began the meal.

"What are you doing wearing a dress?" Kate asked as they proceeded to eat.

"It makes me comfortable," Chris answered taking another helping of casserole. "I've been doing it since grade school."

"That's impossible!" Kate spat out in an immediate reaction. "I would have known!"

The meal progressed and Kate decided she knew the answers, "It's a stress reaction—to all you saw in Afghanistan!" she said.

"No, Mom I've always been this way," Chris protested but it was to no avail.

"It's an escape," she continued. "You'll get through this. It's a stage…"

Later as they were cleaning up the meal she added, "Those heels are really too high. You should dress more conservatively."

Samantha—One Last Try at Marriage

Chris had started dressing as a woman when he was at home after work and on weekends since moving to Tampa. Now that he had his twenty years nearly in, he was finally thinking of leaving the military. He had only another year to go and he was feeling unable to rein his feminine self in anymore.

Now that they knew about his "dressing up" Chris had also taken to dressing as a woman in the evenings when he was in Maryland staying with his family. None of them had acclimated to it or accepted his simple explanatory statements of, "I'm a transgender. Inside I'm a woman." It was too weird and far out for them. His mother still thought it was a reaction to combat trauma and a stage, his father was silent and his sisters continually expressed embarrassment.

"It wouldn't be so embarrassing for you to be gay or trans if you'd been a hairdresser, but you're a SEAL—you're not allowed to do that," Hanna griped. "It will look bad! And what are all my friend going to think? They are going to laugh at you—and me!"

"What about my feelings?" Chris countered. "I've been holding this in for forty years!"

"Just don't dress up here!" Hanna retorted, "What if our friends or neighbors see you like this? We will be mortified. You can't do it!"

"I don't care what a 'friend' of yours thinks about you because of *my* actions!" Chris answered angrily adding, "That's ridiculous, selfish and callous to be worried about what others think and never consider what I think or how I feel."

"Okay, but just go upstairs if anyone comes over!" Hanna begged, rolling her eyes.

"I've been going through this for years now—keeping this bottled up. I'm ready to blow up!" Chris answered fuming inside at his sister's self-centered focus.

His family continued to ignore Chris's newly displayed femininity and asked, "Are you dating anyone? Why don't you get married again?" Chris's father, Luther was intent on Chris pairing up with Samantha, a nice looking family friend around Chris's age who often came around the house. When over one night, he nodded to Samantha and said to Chris, "*She* obviously likes you."

Indeed, Samantha was hanging around a lot since they had met again at a family function. She saw Chris dressed as a woman at home and she seemed accepting of this aspect of his life, even enjoying Chris's feminine side—although she, like the rest of the family, also didn't really seem to grasp that Chris didn't *only* like to dress as a woman—he experienced himself totally as a woman.

She probably thinks she can cure me! Chris cynically thought to himself as he turned his head toward Samantha. She was always hanging around these days and he could see it too—she did like him. And it was obvious his family would be pleased if he married her.

Who am I to be selfish and live the life I want to live? Chris thought later when everyone had gone to bed. *I feel about to explode! But what about their feelings? My sisters, my Mom?* To their faces Chris put on a tough show like he was going to do whatever he needed to—whatever he wanted—but the truth was their feelings did matter to him and so did their judgments.

Maybe I should get married again? Chris thought pondering what everyone wanted him to do: be normal. *It would make things a whole lot easier wouldn't it?* Chris thought, even though deep inside he knew that "normal" for him was impossible. But denial runs deep, as does the desire to be loved and accepted by one's family. And being married would provide a cover in the SEALs as well—no one would need to know his true self. *Why not marry her—she seems to accept me as I am and be cool about me dressing up?* Chris thought as the options twisted about in his mind.

***

The wedding was in January and it was small and presided over by Chris's uncle who was an Archdeacon. His family was so thrilled when Chris told them he'd decided to get married, they put it on for them and paid for everything.

"Good! Now you can settle down and get on with your life," his mother said. He wasn't that messed up after all. Samantha would "cure" him.

Back in Tampa as a newlywed, Chris began "dressing up" all the time except when he went into the office or had to go out to meet contractors or attend official meetings. Samantha was at first cool with it and she enjoyed their nights out to Georgie's and other gay bars dancing together with Chris dressed as a girl—the only places he was safe to be "out" and cross-dressed. They were both trying hard to make it work—but it was a doomed relationship from the start.

After their marriage, Chris tried to satisfy Samantha but he soon realized he couldn't pretend to be the man in their sexual relations. And after two months of trying to make it work with various permutations on a normal sexual life, he shut down and began isolating himself again.

"We never make love anymore!" Samantha complained. She kept asking him to make love—even offered to play the man—but Chris felt it was a trick, and Samantha couldn't understand.

"You knew I liked to dress up! You used to like going to Georgie's dancing together!" Chris reminded her but he could see on her face that she was fed up with it now.

Perhaps it was a shock to Samantha after moving to Tampa with Chris to see in reality how deep his gender issues were. It wasn't just a matter of dressing in female clothes in the evening and on weekends. *He wanted to be a woman!*

Samantha wasn't up for that—she was still in deep denial. And when she begged for a renewal in their sexual relationship Chris felt fear. He already had one failed marriage and two sons that he felt he had neglected during a long career and he knew the avoidance of intimacy with his first wife had driven them apart.

But he also didn't know how to explain to Samantha how he felt—that inside he was a woman and really wanted to be a woman in totality. While he didn't want to repeat the mistakes he'd made with Shelly he could see almost immediately that getting married had been a mistake and that making a graceful exit that wouldn't harm Samantha was going to be difficult to accomplish.

Maybe she's just in it for the money—she's already taken over my Lexus and now she wants to get pregnant! Chris thought in confused panic when they had arguments. *I don't want to make her pregnant on top of all the rest. I've done that already and it was a disaster. I need to get out.*

"This isn't working is it?" Chris asked when one argument got heated. "Maybe we should divorce?"

"We've only been married five months!" Samantha cried out in disbelief.

Samantha was in shock and denial. She had given up her job and upset her entire life to move to Tampa to be with Chris. Perhaps she also believed she could cure Chris and didn't accept the seriousness of his gender issue due to his great male body and Navy SEALs past.

Chris was as incapable of being her husband as she was of curing him. But neither could face that sad truth. They were at a stalemate, and it was painful. Chris turned back to the beer and isolation.

DULLING THE PAIN

Chris would later retire from the military with eighty-percent disability status, suffering pain in his leg referred from nerve damage due to broken vertebrae from when he broke his back and he had pain from when he blew his shoulder out; pain in his arm where the shrapnel had embedded itself; pain in his ankles, elbow and wrists from when he fell through an Afghani roof; and pain in his broken scapula. He was on beer, Vicodin and other pain medications.

"Why can't we just make love? I'm on the pill!" Samantha complained after a night out on the town. They'd been married eight months now and this night they'd both pounded back a bottle of wine and now Chris was heading for the medicine cabinet. *An Ambien should be able to put me to sleep fast enough; just like flying across the world to work in some god forsaken place no American has every heard of.*

"No, it's not a good idea," Chris said washing the pill down. "I'm going to sleep."

"I don't understand you!" Samantha pouted, clicking her high heel shoes on the wood stairs as she followed him up stairs. Chris, brushing his teeth in the bathroom, saw Samantha stand in front of the full-length mirror in their bedroom and pull her dress down off her lithe body. She slipped out of her undies and standing naked in front of the mirror she stared at her breasts—still full and perky, her waist long and slim, her long legs lean and muscular, even longer now as she stood in front of the mirror with only her heels on. Chris could see the thoughts in her head.

Why don't we make love anymore? Samantha asked herself. She knew the answer, but it was too horrible to accept. *He's so handsome, so fucking beautiful and so fucked up! He thinks he's a girl!*

Drunk, she laughed at the thought and throwing back her long hair staggered over to the turn of the century furniture that filled the house. Now standing in front of the chest of drawers she could see only her long hair and smooth breasts in the oval carved wood framed mirror that hung over the chest. Chris got into bed and faced the wall. Samantha put on a pair of shorts and a t-shirt and crawled in next to him and fell asleep.

***

It took a year to make the break with Samantha even though they both knew deep inside after only four months of marriage that it wasn't a marriage—that despite their denial, Chris couldn't be the husband she needed, and Samantha wasn't into being one for him either. The only pulls for her were the paycheck and the honor—it was no small thing to have married a Navy SEAL, and everyone wanted to meet him. Chris was, indeed, charming, and he was climbing up the Pentagon chain of command and had a great future.

On Chris's side, the marriage kept his family happy and kept up appearances for work. But all he thought about was, *I need to be me. I'm not a husband.* And perhaps wondering what kept her in the marriage he began cynically thinking, *She just wants the money. Fuck it, I'm going to quit my job and move to New Zealand if I have to keep up this charade.*

While he saw her as Machiavellian and money-hungry it was likely much more complicated than that—Samantha had entered their relationship believing she could cure Chris and she was deeply shocked and disappointed to find she couldn't. It wasn't easy to take that level of indifference, if not outright rejection. She was hurt and angry. She did have tons of great qualities—just not for him.

After a year they were both ready to call it quits. They went to the court and got a divorce settlement—he would help her with funds to get her back on her feet, and he kept what he had before the marriage.

THE WARRIOR PRINCESS EMERGES

Kristin at Gasparilla in Tampa.

Chris at the Special Operations Forces Mission planning meeting.

Bill Shepherd, U.S. Navy SEAL and the first commander of the International Space Station.

Bill Shepherd gives Chris a retirement plaque that was made in Afghanistan by the guys in the Third Special Forces Group.

Chris at his retirement.

Kristin after coming out in 2013. (photo by Christy Borjes)

Kristin, Anne and Clay in Crystal City.

Kristin in her new work clothes in 2013. (photo by Christy Borjes)

Kristin at the Washington, D.C. Gay Pride Parade.

Kristin enjoys a glass of wine as an "out" woman.

Kristin with sister Lisa.

Kristin on the red carpet.

Kristin dressed and out on the town.

Kristin in Crystal City, 2013.

RETIREMENT & LIVING DOUBLE

Finally in February of 2011, Chris broke free. He had put in his twenty years and it was time to retire. Bill Shepherd gave the retirement speech praising Chris's outstanding and lengthy service in the SEALs to his country. Chris felt honored to have such a man praising him and was humbled as he was "piped" out of the Navy—a longstanding tradition in which Chris departed down the red-carpeted ramp, flags and sailors saluting on both sides, with his shipmates. It's an old tradition symbolic of departing the ship for the last time.

There was a retirement party after the ceremony at Hula Bay, a favorite restaurant and bar for SOCOM people. It was very nicely set up and everyone partied long and hard and had a blast, Chris enjoying the loving well wishes of his SEAL brothers and also relishing the freedom he was about to enjoy to finally embrace his authentic self.

***

I'm free! Chris thought waking up the next morning from his retirement ceremony. *It's time to let the Warrior Princess out!*

Chris had considered living as the woman he felt himself to be for a very long time, but while he was serving as a SEAL he couldn't do it. In the past year without Samantha, he'd been living as a woman at home, but he hadn't taken it to the next step yet—living as a woman at work and he wasn't sure he could.

Now seemed the right time to go for it—to make his body match his identity—or at least start by dressing like a woman in his regular life. And now that he was finally out from the military he could. But would the guys from his former SEAL life accept it? Could he come out as a transgender—as a woman—without giving up everything he had ever worked for in the military and now built an S&T career around?

Afraid to test it, Chris continued his double life—no longer a life that contained inside a "box" that rarely got opened—but a double life in which he lived as a woman at home, out on the town and while he worked from home. But when he went into the office and flew from Tampa up to the Pentagon, Chris still lived as a man and in men's clothing.

Chris had already "come out" as transgender—as Kirstin—at the gay bars in Tampa and in a few other out of town places as well—places where he felt comfortable to be his total self—retired Navy SEAL *and* a woman. But he wasn't yet ready to "come out" entirely at work and among his SEAL brethren. It was his hope to do so but Chris feared the consequences and worried it would harm his career and end in total and complete rejection by the SEALs—something that would be very hard to take after twenty years of serving his country.

FAKE SEALS

"Hey you gotta meet this guy, he's a SEAL too!" the guys at the Red Door bar said as they steered a "faker" Chris's way. Chris had been nursing a drink at a table in one of his favorite out of town bars. He knew the bartenders and they knew he was a retired SEAL—although at the moment Chris was dressed as a woman.

Chris extended his hand. "What BUD/S class were you?"

"BUD/S Class 234," the man replied.

"How was it out on Catalina Island?" Chris quickly added.

Hesitating, the faker replied, "It was like any other class."

Busted.

"Okay so talk to a real SEAL!" Chris said politely. "So why do you want to be me?" Repulsion welled up inside and a desire to punch the guy's lights out. *Why do all these fake tough guys have to pretend their SEALs?* Chris asked himself with anger and pity. *Why do people feel they have to fake someone else's life to be worthy?*

"I *don't* want to be *you!*" the "tough guy" answered, a mix of confusion and disgust crossing his face as he looked at Chris, a "dude in a dress" who was in his tough guy eyes worthy only of disgust.

"But you're saying you want to be a SEAL!" Chris continued. "Where's the glory in that? I've seen death and destruction and *I* don't want to be that!" Chris stormed at the guy, getting angrier by the minute. The faker just stared at him.

What BUD/S class were you in again?" Chris suddenly asked, changing tack.

To this question the guy sputtered and mumbled an inaudible answer—confused and shamed at being caught.

"You're lying! Stop fucking lying! You are lying to everybody here!" Chris shouted at him. "Why do you want to be me? People have died for America—for you to be an asshole? Don't say you're a SEAL to pick up girls at the bar! I'm going to fucking kick the shit out of you!" Chris hollered and, standing there in his dress and high heels, hit the guy, knocking him back. Even as a girl, Chris was still a SEAL and hadn't lost any of "her" combat readiness or aggressive rooting out of evil—in this case, a man who dared to pretend to be an honorable warrior but in reality was just a faker. Instead of fighting back, the fake SEAL ran from the bar holding his jaw to the laughter of everyone watching.

"We always knew he was a fake!" the bartender yelled as the faker suddenly took off.

"We knew he was lying the whole time! That guy is such an asshole! He's kicked out for life from this bar."

Rounds of drinks were bought and Chris laughed as he put back a few more shots to the SEALs who actually were SEALs and served their country, while he sat happily in the bar in a dress and heels.

EXTORTION 17

On August 6th, 2011, thirty-eight people (thirty-one of them Americans, including twenty-two Navy SEALs—most from Dev Group—and five Naval Special Warfare personnel) were shot down in their twin rotor Chinook CH-47 helo while bringing reinforcements to their beleaguered fellow Army Rangers engaged in a fierce firefight against a senior Taliban leader and his commandos.

"I'm so sorry," Janey said as she approached Chris at the memorial service for the killed SEALs. "You knew so many of them, no?" she asked. Chris scanned the room.

Special Warfare Operator Petty Officer 1st Class Aaron C. Vaughn, was one of seventeen Navy SEALs killed in action. Right there across the room was his widow, blonde, blue-eyed Kimberly, a former NFL cheerleader. Aaron was the father of a boy not yet two, and he'd been home for his daughter's birth, only eight weeks ago.

Why did she get the terrible news? He was a great man, a great father. Damn this sucks. Chris thought to himself as he stared across the room at Kimberly.

Chris remembered nearly all of them personally: Jason Workman, married with a wife and twenty-one month old son; Matt Mason, the father of two toddlers, his wife pregnant—he had gone back into the battle even after losing part of his left arm; Darrik Benson, who hadn't yet married the mother of his two-year-old son but planned to; Thomas Ratzlaff, thirty-four leaving behind two sons and his wife pregnant—expecting a daughter; Heath Robinson, thirty-five years old; Luther Douangdara, only twenty-six; Robert Reeves, he had earned four bronze stars; Jonas Kelsall, thirty-three, married for three years; Kraig Vickers, leaving behind a seven-months pregnant wife and two children; Chris Campbell with a fifteen-year-old daughter; Nick Spehar, only twenty-four years old—one of the new guys; Jared Day; John Fass, thirty-one years old; Jon Tumilson; Brian Bill; Kevin Houston; Jesse Pitman; Louis Langlais…

Me and Rat used to ride our motorcycles all over the beach raising hell, Chris reflected as the pain of their deaths clenched at his heart. *Lou was one of my trainers—he was a rock, tough but fair, never flinched.*

Chris Campbell and I did a ton of work together, and ate meals at his house—he was a super stand-up guy. The stories could fill a book about how great these guys were. His mind reeled under the weight of it. *All these amazing guys killed. I can't hold a candle to these guys—taking care of families and friends and living good lives.*

Chris couldn't escape the fact that all his calls home to his boys were short and perfunctory. He couldn't find the way into their hearts. There was too much pain—too much distance between them and he had no idea how to close that gap.

My life is so screwed up with this whole gender thing, Chris thought as his mind returned to the fallen men. *Why them and not me? Nobody would even know I was gone.*

***

After the memorial service, Chris stayed at the family house in Maryland. He wore a black suit with a small trident and Purple Heart pin to the funeral, but back at home, he put his dress back on. His family wasn't happy. "It's odd and someone might see," they continued to say. "What if the neighbors come over?"

"How can you wear a dress when you just returned from being a SEAL and honoring the guys that just died?" his sister asked shaking her head. The rest of the family just went about their business, making believe it would just go away though they constantly worried what anyone else outside the family would think.

Maybe they're right. Chris thought that night as he poured one drink after another for himself. *It should have been me and then I wouldn't have this problem over me anymore.*

PTSD TREATMENT

In his retirement, the Veterans Administration (VA) had assigned Chris to both individual and group therapy for his PTSD, and Kiki, the social worker for his individual sessions, was great. Finally in retirement from the fast pace demands of the SEALs, Chris had the luxury to let his guard down, rest and try to heal his PTSD—as well as finally address his gender issues.

"Whoa, whoa!" Kiki said. "You're talking too fast and not even taking a breath!"

"Sorry," Chris answered sheepishly smiling shyly.

Chris had kept so much locked up inside—so much death, so much pain, so many things he could never talk about, and now in the safety of her warm little office she offered for fifty minutes each week, he let it all pour out.

"I can't keep up!" Kiki explained, unkinking her hands and glancing down at the keyboard she kept handy for notes. "Slow down. You've got plenty of sessions—we'll get to it all."

Chris smiled and slowed it down.

It was comforting finally to have a safe place where he could let it out. The SEALs never admitted to any pain—to anything physical or mental, that could interfere with the mission. They just kept on going. Finally, now he was working through all that pain that had built up over the years and he wanted it out—fast. But Kiki was teaching him that in therapy sometimes slower is faster.

The group therapy was different though, and Chris couldn't stand it. In their doctor-run group, they mixed Vietnam vets—fifty and sixty-year-old bearded guys—with young guys coming back from Afghanistan and Iraq and others who had seen little combat.

"It was really hard being in Germany and seeing all the wounded coming in," one of the vets was saying.

Chris wanted to snort. *You should try being one of them!* he thought.

"When I was a Ranger in Somalia . . . " one of the younger guys started. Chris faded out on what his complaint was. He could hardly keep his concentration in these sessions, he just felt so angry listening to them whining.

"So how was the mountain phase up there in Vermont?" Chris asked the Ranger, testing him to see if he would even know what Chris was referring to.

"It was cold and sucked," the Ranger answered.

He's full of shit! Mountain phase isn't in Vermont—dumb ass! He was probably never in Somalia! The Vietnam guys are even worse with their stories; every Nam vet killed entire villages in one shot and they all got spit on getting off the bus... Chris thought as his anger rose.

Then sure as shit, the Vietnam guy started talking shit about the Army, FTA, and then the Agent Orange stories kicked in. These guys did one tour, then got out of the military, most of them were never in a firefight.

Fucking assholes! Chris, still locked away in his own mind and his own demons, wanted to shout at them. *Have you got any idea what it's like to deploy again and again for thirteen deployments in combat zones where you lose your very own brothers? And there's a ton of SEALs and SF dudes who did twice as much as I did! What are you fucking whining about REMFs? What are you fucking whining about FOBITS?*[8]

"Chris, do you have anything to say?" the doctor running the group session suddenly asked—maybe reading his mind.

"Nothing, I'm fine," Chris answered, "I just need to get away from all this talking."

When the session was over Chris couldn't get out of the room fast enough.

Fuck that! He thought on the way out the door and he didn't come back for any more bullshit faker group therapy sessions.

Hunting

"Let's go deer hunting," Jake, Chris's brother, said over the phone.

It was winter and Chris was home in New York to visit his father and brother. Jake had gotten heavier and was following in his father's earlier life footsteps—drinking too much. Chris was still physically in shape and trained and he could see that Jake was jealous. Jake had always been the natural athlete and now Chris was the fit one and fine-tuned.

Now out in the forest and both dressed as men in deer hunting gear and sitting in two tree stands that Jake had set up that fall, the guys waited for the deer to wander by.

Jake and Luther had both had a few shots earlier in the season—all misses. It was late and nearing sunset, the end of the day of hunting. Chris saw some movement a couple of hundred yards away. He watched through his scope and saw three deer bounding through the forest about a hundred and fifty yards away. He scanned ahead through the thick trees and found a good spot for an ambush to shoot the deer.

He set it up and he watched as one deer crossed his site, two . . . Boom!—his rifle went off as Chris squeezed the trigger. The third deer was in the spot where Chris predicted and it went down.

Jake climbed out of his stand forty yards from Chris and made his way over to Chris's stand.

"I got him," Chris said as Jake was climbing out of the tree.

"No fucking way!" Jake answered. "You didn't even have a shot! It was too far away."

"No he's down—over there," Chris said and taking his gun he began walking determinedly through the trees with Jake following behind.

Maybe it was farther than a hundred and fifty yards, Chris thought as he came to snowy unused service road in the forest. *No, he's over there,* Chris thought after looking back and following with his mind the bullet's trajectory.

"He's across the road," Chris said to Jake as he began trekking across the service road and back into the deeper snow of the forest on the other side. Suddenly Chris saw the buck. Jake saw it too.

"That was a fucking impossible shot!" Jake exclaimed. "How'd you get that shot?"

"Deer are easier than people," Chris answered soberly. Then he bent down and started field-stripping the deer.

Back at home Chris stripped off his hunting attire and dressed again as a woman. It was the first time for Jake to see it and when he walked into the room, he exploded in anger exclaiming, "What the fuck are you doing?"

"It's who I am," Chris answered.

"I don't ever want to see that again," Jake shouted and taking his things stormed out the door. And true to his word, Jake refused to see Chris again.

(Jake later had conversations with Chris and the chasm is healed up. Time does heal the wounds and Jake has even invited Kristin to go hunting this upcoming season.)

CATS IN THE CRADLE

After retirement, Chris was in Tampa and traveling a lot for all of his duties. He still worked with Shep, but he was a contractor now to SO-COM and the Pentagon, employed by Logistics Management Institute as a senior consultant.

Often in the balmy Florida evenings, Chris would sit at home in a dress and think on the patio he had built with friends. He had installed a salt-water fish tank filled with colorful tropical fish and a koi fishpond, and working in his garden and staring at the fish helped him to come to some peace with all the conflicts rolling around inside his mind.

Often in those times—when he sat watching the red, yellow and orange fish darting around in their tank—his thoughts would move to his sons, Max and Henry, and their mother, Shelly.

She was right to leave, Chris thought. *She couldn't handle it.* But sometimes he wondered if they could have made it work—if she could have accepted him as a gender-identified woman and if they could have worked things out sexually as well.

It was too hard for her. She wanted a man, Chris reflected. *And if I could be in a woman's body I guess I'd really prefer to be a normal woman and be with a man,* Chris thought, although those possibilities were so far off in his mind that he hadn't really yet figured out how to best handle his intimate life and how to best express himself sexually.

He never felt anger toward Shelly—she was a good mother to their sons and he was grateful for that. Shelly had taken full custody of the boys and he saw them only once a year—at most. Often he wished it were daily.

They'd like it here, Chris thought and imagined taking them on his sail-boat out on the ocean. *I wish I was a part of their lives!*

The boys were twelve and thirteen now and they still didn't know him.

They'll never be able to accept this, Chris thought looking down at his sundress and girl sandals. *It's bad enough that I wasn't part of their lives—and now they have to accept their father as a transgender?*

It seemed hopeless. *I wish I'd been a normal Dad and stayed!*

But Chris also knew that if he had not faced facts—that he was a transgender individual—and come to grips with that his gender identity was a hundred percent female, everything would have ended badly. Then they really would have no Dad. No more paycheck.

As far as Chris was concerned there was nothing that was going to cure him. He'd tried suppression. He was in therapy. He'd tried marriage. All that was left was blackness and dead ends—and there was still so much to accomplish. There is so much more to do and experience.

Chris needed love. Buddhism maybe—the gentleness and acceptance there appealed to him. He read writings from the Dalai Lama and other works. He read some of the Book of the Dead and many other ancient texts. The search was difficult and uncovered many essential truths that brought him comfort and the will to keep going, but he needed more.

He had to find a way to come to terms with his double life—a man at work and a woman at home. Chris longed to "come out" at work, but he was afraid of losing everything he'd worked for, of the potential condemnation and rejection from his community, and for the shame that he might cause to his brother SEALs. He didn't want to do any harm to anyone—but he also desperately wanted to claim himself as a woman. And he wanted a meaningful relationship in which he could express himself sexually as such. To do that he probably needed to change his body.

Convinced that changing his body was the only real resolution Chris had asked for hormones already at the VA and he'd taken many steps now to begin his transition into womanhood: laser removal of the hair on his face, arms and chest, collagen treatments for his cheekbones, even letting a fake doctor inject silicon into his buttocks to pump them up a bit. He learned how to apply makeup and dress elegantly as a woman.

But it was frustrating and slow moving to make the transition into a female body. The VA wanted to go slow as they worked toward a solution for hormone treatment because while he had been living privately as a woman for nearly two years, he had not transitioned at work. They wanted to be cautious in supporting his change demanding that he "come out" as female in every aspect of his life before they began hormone treatments or offered surgical solutions. To enter back into the SEALs community as a transgender individual would take all his courage and Chris didn't feel strong enough or ready yet to face that.

But Chris also knew if he didn't do something soon he was going to die—or kill himself—the burden of keeping it inside all his life had been too much. He was exhausted from it and couldn't pack it up and make it go away any longer. The "inner girl" was screaming to come out. And if he wanted to stay alive, Chris had to find answers.

***

The healing Chris was seeking was slow in coming, but it was opening up finally in many areas of his life and he also wished to support the healing of others who like himself came home from war wounded in one way or another. Chris began to draft the idea for a nonprofit organization—the Healing Grounds—a garden center and place to help wounded warriors and returning vets by organizing their lawn and garden care and giving them support to heal.

Likewise healing was happening in the family. In the past decade, Luther who had given up drinking years before and softened over the years, began reaching out to Chris—writing e-mails about books he was reading, issues, problems he encountered and his life's journey:

HOW'S YOUR LIFE GOING- YOU HAVE HAD AN AMAZING ADVENTUROUS LIFE SETTING NEW BENCHMARKS---ALL OVER THE WORLD--MET HIGH LEVEL PEOPLE---GOT TO BE A TOUGH ADJUSTMENT AT TIMES--

I KNOW WE NEVER HAD THAT LEVEL OF COMMUNICATION BUT IF YOU EVER HAVE A NEED TO TALK THE TALK I AM A GOOD LISTENER AND NOT JUDGEMENTAL--

DON'T READ ANYTHING INTO THIS---IT'S JUST I NEVER HAD THAT LEVEL OF COMMUNICATION WITH MY DAD--WISH I DID---NOT PRYING JUST OFFERING--I LOVE YOU SON---DAD

***

CHRIS-----SORRY---LONG TIME NO COMMUNICATE---ALWAYS SAY I'LL GET BETTER---NEED TO---TIMES RUNNING OUT---AND YOU ARE VERY IMPORTANT TO ME---ALWAYS IN MY PRAYERS--KEEP ME IN THE LOOP---

GOOD SUMMER--LOT GOING ON--YOUR SISTER'S MOVE--A NEW CAREER FOR YOU--MAYBE MOM'S LAST YEAR--NEW CHALLENGES FOR ME--IN MY NEW TUTORING ENDEAVORS--KEEP IN SHAPE--VISIT YOU--BUILD A MAN CAVE--FINISH MY HISTORY--BEAT TOM IN GOLF--TRY TO UNDERSTAND FEMALE SPEAK--NEVER--

GLAD I BROUGHT YOU ALONG FOR THIS TRIP LOVE PAPA

***

CHRIS----WAS HUNTING THIS AFTERNOON---SITTING ON A BANK---OVERVIEW OF THE VALLEY----A WARM DAY---THINKING OF YOU AND YOUR NEW VENTURE OFTHE HEALING GROUNDS---AND THE RAMIFICATIONS THAT IS COULD HAVE ON YOU AND THE OUTREACH TO HOME COMING VETS---SEEMS LIKE THIS COULD BE JUST WHAT THE DOCTOR ORDERED FOR THEM AND YOU---KEEP ME IN THE LOOP---I WANT TO BE PART OF THE PROJECT---OH YES I WAS AT COUSING MARY'S FOR DINNER AND WAS TALKING TO HER DAUGHTER AND HUSBAND SASHA---THEY WERE KEENLY INTERESTED IN WHAT YOU ARE DOING---I WILL SEND THEIR BLOG OR WEB PAGE---

ALWAYS ON MY MIND-LOVE PAPA

***

When Chris showed Anne these obviously loving e-mails he explained, "He's not the same man he was when I was growing up. Today my Dad is a warm-hearted man who over the years has learned many lessons."

Like father, like son. Chris also has learned many lessons. They each have their painful histories, as do many people around the world living life and attempting to do better. They each try to communicate and each have their unique ways and sometimes it still misses, but they are trying.

Chris called it an "impedance mismatch", an electrical engineering term. Nowadays, Chris enjoys the time he has with his father. Luther still doesn't "like" Kristin, but he is accepting and trying to understand. Luther says, "Chris was my son and I don't want to lose my son."

THE MISFIT MANSION

Things were looking up for Chris. After so many years of demanding service when he literally never had time for himself and could avoid the inner conflict with the pressure building and building, Chris was in retirement and finally free to address the gender issue. He now had the time and help to do so—and he was also finding society becoming much more accepting to his issue. In his psychotherapy sessions with Kiki, Chris was working through his traumatic bereavement from all the death and destruction he witnessed and years of built-up painful thoughts, as well as his gender issues. Kiki was warm, accepting and smart and he felt safe with her.

His home had become his sanctuary, a place where he had installed a large patio, built a koi pond and inserted a saltwater aquarium filled with colorful fish into his outdoor bar. He loved to sit quietly and mediate and find an inner peace. And he continued to work on the Healing Grounds, the nonprofit he started to help other wounded warriors heal in a similar manner through gardening and rest.

Chris spent his mornings in a sundress, sipping coffee and peacefully feeding his fish, watering the plants and throwing peanuts to the squirrels. At nights he could switch on a light on the aquarium and be mesmerized by the multicolored fish.

"I'm starting a foundation," he told Kiki. "It's called the Healing Grounds, and it's for vets like me that come home wounded or messed up and they maybe can't mow their lawns or they can't take care of things because they have mental or physical problems upon re-entry. I put a bid in on a property and if I get it for the foundation we'll have a green house for growing plants and places for vets to stay while they get their heads on straight."

Chris rescued a pit bull mutt from the Humane Society and he started to rescue people as well. He offered a room in his home to Pete, a friend of a teammate he met that was out of luck and need a place to live a room temporarily, in exchange for general upkeep like weeding, watering the plants, feeding the fish and taking care of the dog while he was away on short trips. Then he offered Teddy, a retired Green Beret who was just out of the military and going to school on the GI Bill, a place to stay in his "granny apartment" above his garage. Teddy mowed the lawn in lieu of rent. Last to arrive in his home—the "Misfit Mansion" as Chris took to calling it due to its odd assortment of those who were temporarily housed and fed—was a friend from Canada named Amie whose boyfriend had just abruptly broken up with her.

Having a need for a "family" of sorts, Chris accepted the misfits for all their problems and enjoyed that they all accepted him as a "girl". "Misfit Mansion" was now full and having surrounded himself with acceptance, Chris was starting to feel stronger.

In December of 2012, Chris's colleagues confronted him about drinking too much. He mostly drank to fall asleep and get over the pain that covered nearly his entire body. It also helped him sleep past the bad dreams. When they took him to task over it, Chris pushed away any defensiveness and thought, *It's good to have close friends to help me through the bad times and tell me the truth.* He promised Shep to cut way back; and he did. He still had pain—everywhere in his body—but Ibuprofen could keep it within bearable range. And as he began to embrace the female self, Chris also felt for once in his life genuinely happy and at peace about life.

BODY IMAGE

I want to cut it off! Chris thought as he showered. *It's not part of my body! It's not part of me!* He'd really thought about cutting it off once—he had the courage to do it—but he knew better than to do something like that. He knew he'd bleed out and die. The only way to get rid of it was to do the operation. He felt such self-loathing for the male body he was trapped in that he punched the shower wall a few times.

I need to come out, he thought in desperation, *and do the hormones and the surgery!* But coming out in public—letting everyone know—it was risky. *Would the SEALs accept it? Could he keep working? Would the whole world—not just his family—reject him outright?* His family was okay when it was hidden—but it was clear they were not okay with coming out in public. It caused them too much shame and that was all they could focus on—never able to empathize with how painful it was for Chris to keep this essential part of his self suppressed.

As Chris worked on figuring out how to express his identity as a woman, he began wearing female clothes everywhere but to work. He got pedicures and, when he knew he'd be at home for a bit, manicures as well, and he slowly built up his new female wardrobe.

Chris also reached out to the transgender community and made friends with other men who "dressed up" or who felt their true identity was female, including ex-navy and marines and many others. For Chris meeting these other transgender friends was like coming out of desert to find fresh water. Teri, a truck driver by day and a very good-looking woman at night, took Chris under "her" wing and invited Chris along with some of the other "T-girls" for nights out on the town. Being able to be "herself", Kristin felt wonderful and supported as week after week the "T-girls" met at Georgie's or some of the other gay hot spots in the area—safe places where most people didn't stare and Kris felt accepted. Finally, she was finding a much needed support network along with loads of love and acceptance.

Chris learned how to put on make-up—the many tricks that men who want to dress as women need to learn: that rubbing red lipstick into his chin and cheeks could neutralize the five o'clock shadow and how to keep it hidden under foundation. He learned to place white powder strategically under his eyes, down his nose and on his cheekbones and dark powder in the hollows of his cheeks and along his nose to create a sculptured, more feminine face.

Though Chris was proud of his newfound skills, at home with his family, Chris's sister Hanna commented, "Normal girls don't wear that much make up," she said. "You look like RuPaul!"

"Hanna, I'm a dude and have a beard; thanks a lot for the help," Chris answered, but thinking how beautiful RuPaul was, he smiled inside at the compliment.

In anticipation of going the whole way—transitioning into a female body through hormones and a sex change, Chris began to take the first steps.

He finished up the laser removal of his beard, arm and chest hair so that very little of it grew back, and he learned how to shave his legs. He found a great little shop down the street to give him acrylic nails and opted for an elegant French mani-pedi, though he removed them when he needed to go into the office.

In terms of dress, Chris was initially a bit like an adolescent girl, enamored by bling, high sparkly platform shoes and short sparkly dresses—anything that screamed female sexuality—but keeping in mind his sisters' elegant and stylish ways, he calmed down. Except for a few short dresses for the bar scene, he chose more elegant dresses for evening and informal sundresses for running around town.

He found a plastic surgeon to inject collagen into his cheekbones to fill them out to look more feminine. Slowly he was moving into his female body, creating congruence between the inside and the out.

GASPARILLA

It was January of 2013, and the city of Tampa was putting on its annual Gasparilla festival, restaging the "invasion" of Jose Gaspar, the legendary Spanish nobleman and naval officer who had turned to piracy and supposedly sailed from a secret island base south of Tampa and plundered ships in the Gulf of Mexico. To celebrate Gaspirilla, Tampa residents dressed as pirates. Chris was among them, decked out festively in a velveteen coat, pirate breeches and sporting a real antique British pistol (purchased in Afghanistan at the bazaar), a girl's wig and high heels.

Chris started out partying with friends, but as the night wore on he got separated from them and ended up on his own. Four hours into heavy drinking, Chris's make-up started to fade and he began to look more and more like a "dude in a dress". Looking for the place to finish out his night, Chris took a taxi to Ybor City and when he got out of the taxi he ran across four other drunk "pirates" on the sidewalk—young twenty-something year-old African Americans.

"Arrgh maties!" Chris called out, drunkenly greeting them as he turned his body sideways to pass through the foursome.

Seeing he wasn't a girl but a man in a dress, the four boys stood solid and blocked Chris from passing, and one punched Chris hard in the face, knocking him off his high heels. Once on the ground, the others then began kicking and beating Chris, jumping up and down on his legs and ankles.

Chris groaned as he sat up. Dimly through the shock of the assault and slowed by his drunken haze, Chris saw that his wig was flung off, laying some ways away on the street, and his handbag and all the things in it were strewn about as well. He made his way down to a bar that he frequented. The bartender, Richard, and bouncer, Josh, were angry they couldn't have prevented the incident from happening. And there was something very ironic, Chris thought, about black kids attacking him for being a "minority". *Fucking prejudiced bigots.*

Briefing with the Deputy Assistant Secretary of Defense & Meeting Anne

It was the last day in January 2013 and freezing cold when Anne emerged from the subway for a counter-terrorism meeting at the U.S. State Department and she was hurrying—trying not to be late—but after taking a wrong turn she saw that she'd have to backtrack.

Anne, a counter-terrorism researcher and an adjunct professor in the Psychiatry Department at Georgetown University Medical Center, had been living out of the country for thirteen years —living in Belarus, Belgium and Greece—following her U.S. Ambassador husband's career and doing research on her own. She was still re-acclimating to Washington, D.C.—not doing so well this day. Anne eventually found the building and relieved to get out of the cold, hurried up the elevator to the eighth floor where she came to the meeting check-in table.

"Has it started?" Anne asked.

"Yes," the young woman sitting there nodded and handed over her nametag.

"Are you serving wine?" Anne asked with a big smile crossing her face as she eyed the long-stemmed glass of red wine sitting beside the woman.

"Yes!" the woman smiled back and pointed to a nearby doorway, "You can go to the buffet first—take something—and then go right on in. They started about ten minutes ago."

Pouring herself a generous glass of Merlot and filling a plate with crab cakes and tuna sandwiches, Anne carried both to the conference room not realizing she was entering from the front of the room—near the lecterns.

"Here, sit here," Bonnie Green, the director of the conference said in a low voice as she rose and smiling kindly showed Anne to a chair right in the front. Bonnie pulled the "reserved" sign from it and took Anne's glass of wine while she unbundled from her coat and scarf and got settled in. Windswept hair, bright red cheeks and laden with a glass of wine Anne, saw that a few of the participants were glancing at her and smiling. Anne blushed and then smiled back mischievously—it was so great to come out of the cold and be offered a nice glass of red wine, snacks *and* to sit down right in front to listen to engaging speakers.

Sipping her wine she settled in and caught up with the speakers. They had just started and the Pentagon's Assistant Secretary of Defense Ben Riley was giving a talk on current activities concerning Irregular Warfare and Science and Technology. Soon renowned counter-insurgency researcher Dr. David Kilcullen took the stage. Last on the roster of speakers was a young looking retired Navy SEAL, Chris Beck, who was slated to speak on the topic of The Future of Irregular Warfare.

I should ask Chris for an interview, Anne thought as she listened to Dr. Kilcullen's talk. Anne had been asked by a colleague in the Navy SEALs to help with a study of psycho-social resilience amongst the SEALs.[9] The Navy SEALs Foundation had gotten involved to help with funding given the military didn't have enough resources, but they also were taking forever to set her up to begin the interviews that everyone had agreed were important.

Just start—you know you can create a network of interviewees fast and that's the way you've always done things—not waiting around for bureaucratic wheels to turn, Anne mused as she listened to the speaker.

As she was thinking, Anne noticed the SEAL, Chris Beck, looking at her. Probably she was the only one in the room who had dared bring their glass of wine into the conference. Anne smiled at Chris and he smiled back as she continued to sip her wine.

When Chris got up to speak he took an active stance—different from the speakers who'd gone before. He moved the lectern to the side and began to enthusiastically extrapolate on the former and new dimensions of warfare.

Explaining that the old military acquisitions system of buying tanks and ships was fast becoming obsolete to some of the new challenges, Chris lectured, "It's *now* about making this tank or warrior invisible throughout *all* of the spectrums and how to fight an ideology that is based upon myth and dogma! It's *now* about how to deal with a weapon that can be produced on a 3-D printer with no serial numbers or tracking of any kind—how to deal with the narco traffic of synthetic drugs printed in my garage! I don't need to smuggle drugs in from overseas anymore! I can print whatever I need right at home! What gun law is going to stop someone from 'printing' an AK47 out of exotic material in his own basement?"

As he pointed and gestured with his arms and paced across the front of the room, Chris had the audience rapt—they knew he'd been on the front lines and he knew what he was talking about.

"The entire Pentagon is caught in the past," Chris warned. "Now irregular warfare exists *in the Cloud!* So much of what we are going to be battling is in the non-physical world. It's a totally new kind of war! It's a war of ideas and innovations, ideology and fanaticism. Their network is light and fast and in the cloud while our network is stuck on NMCI or other massive dinosaur systems. We are still building tanks for the Fulda Gap; they are building ideas and a massive brainwashed following of adherents." Chris continued, "If we do not change how we are doing the 'business of war' we will become obsolete. The Departments, "Defense, State and Aid" need to align and work together in a whole of governance approach. The departments must work with industry and we need to drastically streamline the acquisition process for the 'smaller programs' and below. You will see this in my hand out for later reference." Chris amusedly added, "I work in the big building with five sides if you need to speak in more detail on any of these subjects."

Anne had a strong intuitive sense—and it usually showed itself when she got into a free form, unstructured space or when she was deeply connected with another person in an interview or in therapy—and she recognized that she was in that weird intuitive space now too. It was a space and a skill she had used often in her work searching out and interviewing terrorists during her field research. When it was active she often just knew the right persons to approach or the right questions to ask.

Feeling this was one of those moments, Anne didn't worry when the presentations ended. She knew she would approach Chris to ask for an interview—and she somehow knew down to the core of her being that he wouldn't be leaving if she took the time to go refill her wine glass—that she'd get the interview.

"I liked your comments after the presentation," a retired Army Green Beret named Dave told Anne. "So what do you do?" Dave asked.

"I just finished writing a book—it's about a decade of interviewing terrorists," she answered. "But now I'm working on a resilience study for the Navy SEALs. I'd like to ask our last speaker for an interview. " She explained the purpose of the study was to explore through in-depth interviews how the SEALs dealt with issues of PTSD, and the stress of the lengthy and frequent tempo of combat deployments. "These are some amazing characters and I won't be surprised if in addition to distress, many of them have also come up with some great coping strategies," Anne summarized. "I should probably go ask our speaker now, before he leaves," she added.

"I know Chris well," Dave replied concern crossing his face. "He's had a bad case of PTSD and working on coping. It's hard to say if it's working."

"Oh, I'm sorry to hear that," Anne reflected.

"Let me find him and introduce the two of you," Dave offered and he led Anne out into the hallway where Chris was standing. Anne already felt they'd met and she knew she would be interviewing him—her unshakable inner knowledge resounded.

"Hi," Anne said, shaking Chris's hand and not letting it go—a very uncharacteristic move for her but it felt right now. "I'm working for the SEALs on a resilience project and I'd like to ask if I could interview you one day about those type of issues. I know you saw me across the room and you already know you can trust me—don't you?" she asked smiling, finally releasing his hand.

"Yes, I do trust you," Chris nodded and smiled warmly. She was right—somehow they had already connected. Dave bowed out, and Chris and Anne ducked into a doorway to an office and stood inside talking for a bit.

"Dave said you were struggling with PTSD and getting over a divorce," Anne told him.

"Yeah, but that's done now." Chris admitted somewhat sheepishly. They spoke for some time and then Chris suddenly offered, "I also have a gender identity disorder," Then pulling out his phone and scrolling through the pictures, he showed them to Anne.

"That's me," he said, pointing to a nice-looking dark haired woman in a dress. It was Chris—in a wig and dressed as a woman. Blinking in disbelief, Anne smiled and looked into his face. He wasn't laughing—he was serious.

"I'm looking for someone to help me write my book, I have a lot to say and I think there are people this book could really help. Are you a writer?" Chris asked.

"I can write," Anne answered, slowly considering, "But I'd only write your book if it was something that was good for you and if you were healthy. I wouldn't want to do anything that might bring harm to you. Are you sure you want to tell *this* story *now*?" Anne worried that maybe Chris would be ruining his career by letting something like that out in public—*a Navy SEAL coming out as transgender would likely make a stir!*

"Yes, I want to put this book out now. There are many people out there with similar problems. They have no mentors and sometimes no hope. They are lost. I would like to help," Chris answered, resolute.

"Let's pick a time to meet again when you are free," Anne offered. "We've all had some wine and it's late, but let's meet and we can do that interview and talk if you like about writing your book."

"How's tomorrow lunch?" Chris asked.

Anne smiled and agreed.

BUILDING TENSION

"Do nothing to discredit or dishonor the brotherhood.*"**

—Portion of the Navy SEAL code of honor

Driving down Crystal Avenue in Crystal City, Arlington not far from the Pentagon, Anne turned on 19th checking her phone for the directions. Seeing the row of restaurants and bars she slowed down to check their numbers. Locating Freddie's—a bar with a Caribbean look to it, she quickly parked and then hustled into the back entrance.

Anne hadn't noticed that the whole front of the building was draped in rainbow colored banners and was obviously a LGBT (Lesbian, Gay, Bi-sexual, Transgender) restaurant.   She scanned the tables, then not seeing Chris, she searched along the bar until her eyes lit on him sitting on a barstool at the bar—tastefully dressed as an elegant woman in a wig, medium-length striped knit skirt, shirt and high heels.

"Hi!" she said running up to him. "I'm sorry I'm late!" she added placing her notebook down on the bar and taking a seat next to Chris and trying to acclimate to this new vision of the SEAL she'd met the day before. And then noticing his plate with a few sweet potato fries left on it she asked, "Did you eat already?"

Anne decided to just take Chris's appearance in stride without commenting and to listen and learn where this meeting was going, "So you want to write a book?" she asked after a bit taking up her pen thinking that's as a good a place to start as any other. "Tell me how this all got started."

"I knew I was a girl in third grade," Chris explained and they took off with Chris going back into his childhood and Anne asking questions.

"As a young child, I'd dream of switching bodies with my sister. I'd go to bed thinking, *I want to be her!* And I'd wake up in the morning thinking *Oh my God it came true!* Then, feeling totally that I was a girl, I'd see I was still in a boy's body. I was devastated."

"My psychologist, from the VA (Veterans Administration) that I have been seeing since retirement has already diagnosed me with gender identity disorder," Chris explained and then waxing philosophical asked, "But is there a pure gender? Are any of us purely male or female or is it all gray and mixed up? Does the "Maker" have a gender? If we have to define, I know I'm way more female, just not showing well on the outside." He smiled.

They talked for another hour or so while Chris also opened up about the challenges of experiencing himself as a female but being caught in a male body *and* the significant psychological and physical challenges of figuring out how to make that work in society, the military or even while partnering up with someone in a committed relationship.

"I don't want to be alone the rest of my life," Chris remarked as he glanced down the bar at the drag queen taking the microphone to sing Karaoke. "I don't want to wait until I'm as old as her to come out. And also I'm not a gay guy looking to hook up with a guy. If I have to define myself, it comes close to a straight girl!"

This is something that confuses nearly everyone. Not gay? A straight woman? Chris explained, telling Anne that she now calls herself Kristin. "I have many friends in the LGBT community; I have come to love and respect many of them and they do the same for me. But my male friends in this community like their lovers as men and enjoy that company and I want to be a regular woman from down the street—so that doesn't fit.

I'm just trying to close the chasm between being a "man" and becoming the woman that I feel I am. And I'm not really tied to having a mate in any form right now—I'm just growing into my new life," Kristin explained.

"It's very difficult and most of the time I feel alone on this path," Kristin continued. "And the more people try to figure it out or stereotype it, the worse it gets. I just want to be with my friends and grow as a person. As RuPaul says 'How can you love anyone else if you don't love yourself?' I'm learning to love myself!"

Anne nodded. This wasn't a world she was familiar with, so she continued to listen, trying to take it all in. And Anne found even in her short time listening and observing that here was a lovely human being, filled with empathy and kindness.

"Anyway, who likes *a guy* in a dress?" Kristin continued the thought and laughed sadly, pondering the difficulties of making a relationship with

someone who would see her as the woman she experienced herself to be—
on the inside at least.

"Gays guys like me as a friend but don't want to be with me. I'm not
part of their world. I'm really a straight girl—like this," Kristin continued as she ran her hand over her indicating her female attire—including a
tasteful bust line. Her hand came to rest on the bar as she toyed with the
elegant silver clutch lying on the bar. "I'm just a girl, that's all. I want to
be a normal girl and live a normal life as a woman."

Anne nodded, taking in the black wedge boots, opaque tights, elegant
knit striped skirt falling to his knees and blue high cut blouse. Tasteful silver earrings peeked out beneath his smartly cut brunette wig. Aside from
his height, muscled shoulders and strong hands, Chris could pass as a nice
looking and well-dressed woman. The only edgy thing in his attire was a
long black and white printed cotton scarf that Chris intermittently played
with and then rearranged again to fall over his shoulders. It was printed
with a pattern of skull and bones—perhaps reminiscent of the emblem of
the SEAL Team squadron.

"If I went home with one of these guys they would just want to do some
S&M routine with me dressed up in a prostitute outfit, and that's not me
at all." Chris continued looking about the gay bar. "I don't like to dress in
slutty or sexy clothes. That's not me! I want to dress like my sisters—elegant and smart."

"So *how do* you work this out sexually?" Anne asked.

"I don't want to be a guy in a dress—a freak show. I want to be a girl!
I want to be pretty. Just a regular girl down the street—white picket fence.
Well maybe not a white fence—maybe a big garage with my welder, a beer
fridge and a Harley and a big garden out back," Chris explained, laughing. "I'm not into fetish scenes, swinging or stuff like that. It seems that
everything gets stereotyped into the most base element and I don't think I
fit into any categories," Chris said.

"So what will you do?" Anne persisted.

"I have to change my body and then find someone that is willing to be
with me—as a woman," Chris explained. "I just want to be in a couple—
two human beings with total acceptance."

"Were you married before?" Anne probed.

"Yes—twice," Chris answered, sadness and a look of tiredness crossing his face. "I was married to my first wife for nine years. We'd literally
been on three dates and she got pregnant on the fourth. She talked about

many options other than marriage, but I told her, 'No let's do the right thing.' She reluctantly agreed."

"We got married and then two days later I was in Bosnia in that war. I didn't ever give her a fair shake," Chris continued a deep grief filling his voice, "and my two sons didn't know me at all. I was *never* home—I was just a paycheck to them! She was totally loyal, a great wife and a great mother. I could never tell her how sorry I am for that." A grimace of deep pain crossed his face as he lowered his eyes and sat silent for a moment. When he lifted them they were filled with tears. "It kills me they are without a Dad up in Minnesota." He stared off into space for a few more minutes, and Anne waited for the grief to pass and then changed the subject to offer some relief:

"How did you make it through the SEALs if you felt you were a woman the whole time? Wasn't that hard?"

"No, not always, I was raised by a father who was a football coach. I was raised to be tough. I was beaten on one side of my head with a Bible and the other side with a football cleat! It was because of football and my own psyche—I didn't care if I was killed, it didn't matter to me. I was living in a blackness and my basic feeling was 'Fuck it!'"

"You wanted to die?"

"No, not really. Sometimes in the past. Not at all now. I love where I am going, I am happy. But there were a lot of SEALs that were spooked by me. I was too intense. On the tours I was going full steam with reckless abandon—it's not always a good thing. I was usually on my own, alone as a bearded local warlord doing my job. I was the guy way out with the locals or up in the hills all by myself. I would set up stuff for the real team guys, who were in the squadrons all gunned up, to come in and kick in the doors, kill or capture the enemy. But, when we did get into firefights I'd be yelling, 'Come on motherfuckers, is that all you got?' I got kinda intense sometimes.

"Even in BUD/S, my internal fortitude was over the top. I didn't care how far I could push this human shell because I didn't like my shell! The biggest thing was, I was trying to turn off my gender problem by being Superman [in the SEALs]. I also might have gotten married thinking I could turn it off." Chris looked down in shame at his striped knit skirt

"You were raised religious?" Anne asked going back to his comment about his father being a football coach with a Bible.

"Yes and the religious aspect is difficult," Chris admitted. "I was raised Lutheran, then Baptist. But seriously think about it; God is not sexual—not male or female. My soul is energy," Chris explained, looking for some confirmation that he wasn't a horrible sinner.

Anne smiled, nodding.

"I'm just stuck in a man's body now and I wait to be a woman—but really in the end we are all energy and part of the Great Tapestry. If me becoming a woman now in this life makes me "more whole" and happier within my skin, wouldn't that be good for my energy and everyone's energy in general? Wouldn't that make everyone around me better and happier and gain energy off me? I can do real good now—on earth today—but I need to heal myself and make myself whole. Get closer to the Maker."

"It sounds rough," Anne remarked. "A lot of people will have trouble accepting it. How is your family taking it?"

"My brother refuses to see or talk to me," Chris explained. "I last talked to my Dad a few months ago, probably not his fault, and now my mother is mad at me due to an argument over the gender issue with my sister. One of my sisters punched me in the mouth the last time we saw each other. And my Mom's kind of disowned me due to her favoring that sister. She says I'm drinking too much, but I feel like I'm always pretending, hiding who I really am. And if I'm my real self, I feel like everyone wants me to go away!

"Can you imagine always having to pretend?" Chris asked plaintively, looking Anne in the eyes. She felt he was searching for any affirmation he could find as a human being—any sense of self worth he could find in the eyes of others. "I was in the SEAL teams! That's what I was for 20 years and that's all anyone wants. I feel like my family and everyone want me to go around like Popeye, dancing with my big bulging arms on my sides," Chris explained as he parodied a Popeye dance—his eyes full of sadness despite the joking.

"I have nobody! I was fucking lonely all my life—although the SEALs were good," Chris added a gleam lighting up in his eye as he recalled the deep and abiding camaraderie of "the brotherhood".

"Was it ever an issue in the SEALs when you felt you were a woman inside?" Anne asked.

"No, never," Chris answered immediately—with no hesitation in his voice. His face becoming serious he continued, "I never pursued any part of my femme life while a SEAL; kept it locked up." Chris went on, "It's not bodies out there anyway. It's surreal and you enter an animal instinct in which you feel 'I will defend my friends to the end of time'. The bond of brotherhood is so strong! It was at a spiritual level. It was just us, as spirits fighting together, and a lot of us died," Chris said, his eyes staring downward as his voice again fell in sadness.

Anne waited in silence, honoring the dead with him.

"In a way it's pretty ironic that I was fighting the Taliban in Afghanistan," Chris started again after a few moments. "They are the worst women haters in the world and *I was a woman the whole time!*" Chris remarked laughing at the paradox of it.

"It was weird that I could grow a beard and trick them into thinking I was one of them—and really *I'm an Amazon woman in disguise as a U.S. military guy in disguise as a Pashtun!* Weird that *I was really a woman* fighting for their freedom! If they see a girl reading, they'll shoot her or chop her up and feed her to the goats. Their general attitude against women made me just hate them even more!

"This whole thing has been so hard all my life. I feel my psychological age is only eighteen or twenty," Chris added—his real age was forty-six. "I'm just figuring it all out now." Anne listened and continued to take notes as they talked. It wasn't the SEALs interview she had been expecting—but he'd warned her and showed her the pictures of himself as a woman the day before.

"There's a sports bar next door," Chris said. I want you to see what that's like for someone like me."

Walking in alongside Chris, Anne indeed got a taste of what his world was like: people looked up in the usual way and looked them both over but then did a short double take on Chris, trying to get a bead on whether he was a man or a woman. Chris just smiled and nodded while a few people gawked as together they found a table in the back of the bar where they could continue conversing.

"My father used to take my brother and me to the bars when we were just toddlers on the weekends and lock us in the car while he went inside to drink," Chris recalled. "He'd crack the window and leave us in the car while he got liquored up."

"Was he a drunk?" Anne asked.

"No, but he did drink. He used to give Budweiser to the pigs on our farm—they loved to drink Bud. I like Sam Adams myself. He was a patriot-brewer, you gotta dig that," Chris joked changing the subject. "My dad was a schoolteacher and a football coach and very controlled in that regard. So he only drank on weekends, but I guess he was a binge drinker. Then the sometime in the eighties he quit totally. I've only seen him have a glass of wine once or twice since the mid eighties."

"My brother was blonde and very athletic—a natural," Chris said thinking back again to his childhood and the forces that shaped Chris's psyche. "He was always favored by my father. I was always the jackass and couldn't explain why I'd done what I did. I was the black sheep. My brother was never wacked by the belt. I was the bad one and got the belt."

Anne nodded surprised that he could discuss family violence so openly already. Usually it took awhile for people to own up to such experiences—most tended to suppress or deny such memories. Although they had been sitting with drinks in front of them for a long time—maybe the alcohol and late hour also made it easier to open up.

"I was the only one in the entire family who was hit," Chris explained a pained expression crossing his face as he remembered. "I always told the truth and spoke out, even to my own demise. And I was the only one tough enough to take it, I guess."

"Did he *actually* beat you?" Anne asked, as she didn't want to record his father as "abusive" if in fact he hadn't been. "What did he use?"

"No, he paddled me with a paddle or the belt. It wasn't that bad or that often. I deserved it most likely—I goofed around a lot. I was a wild kid." Chris said. Anne thought he was blaming himself as many abuse victims usually do.

Chris did not seem to be exaggerating, and his pain over whatever had happened was obvious. And it was also clear that Chris was reliving it from time to time as he retold it to Anne; she could see that at times his face would fill with pain and he needed a break, needed to change the conversation from time to time because it was so emotionally painful to recount.

"I'd be lying in the fetal position on the floor," Chris explained pulling his arms up over his face and head as if to ward off blows, "and I'd be thinking *I just want to be a girl!*"

To Anne it sounded like Chris had responded to his father's scapegoating and violence by slipping into a female gender identity—or the wish to be female at least—as a somewhat dissociated self, a female self that he believed would be both safe and loved.

"I hate myself for not being pretty—for not being prettier. I wanted to be a girl so badly," Chris explained speaking of how the mismatch between his inner self and the outer body was so painful. "I'm very embarrassed of my [lack of] boobs, of my body."

"Do you think maybe due to your childhood experiences you got beauty and love confused? That you think beauty will make you loveable?"

"I don't know," Chris answered, pain crossing his face. "Why was my Dad so mean to the boys?"

"Did you keep the two sides of yourself separate?" Anne asked curious to understand how much the female side was a dissociated self.

"No, it was always there, the main part of me really," Chris answered. Indeed it sounded as if once his female gender identity was in place, it was always there and Chris was constantly aware of his inner self as a girl that didn't match his outer male self. "I tried to shut it down, disavow it," Chris explained, "but it was impossible. I just lived asexual for the longest time. I kept my femme bottled up. It was easier…and safer.

"I had no wife love, I had no sexual love, I had no brotherly love—I pushed it all away," Chris said explaining how despite his bonds to his SEALs brothers he never truly let anyone into his emotions. "I closed everything down my entire life. I closed my sexuality down," he explained as a look of infinite sadness filled his face. "My wife would say, 'Chris never loved me', but it's not true. I didn't love myself—I didn't know what love was or how to treat it. I just wanted to be a girl so badly and have someone love me like that.

"You should write my story with me," Chris said looking at the volumes of notes Anne had already amassed from their two nights of talking. "Are you free?" he asked and Anne nodded answering:

"Yes, I'm between projects right now. I've been waiting for this SEALs project to get going. That's why I asked you for an interview in the first place—to get that rolling," she explained.

Chris invited Anne to come down to Tampa and stay with him for a week or longer and observe him in his regular life where he could relay more stories and memories.

"You can stay at the 'Misfit Mansion'," Chris offered, explaining that he owned a home and that he had opened his doors to three others who were also struggling with PTSD or other life traumas.

"You know," Anne began as she tried to think of a way to diplomatically point out to Chris that he didn't seem to have good boundaries.

"I have no boundaries!" Chris said cutting through her thoughts. "I don't give a fuck about boundaries! Why should I? I should be dead! Cats have nine lives—I've already used up twelve! Why should I care about boundaries?"

Anne laughed. It was funny to consider why emotional and relational boundaries might be protective for someone who had spent all his life learning assault methods and ways of keeping himself safe in the harshest of circumstances. *Maybe he didn't need boundaries after all, but then again maybe he did,* she thought listening to him.

"Okay, I'll come to Tampa," Anne answered smiling in response to his mix of innocence and pain. "I'll write your story with you."

"I'm not a man," Chris repeated as they finished that night off. "I can count on one hand how many women I've been with," he explained trying to make his point that he tried to be with women, but it didn't work because inside his head he was one.

"I want to come out as soon as possible. If I can't start hormones soon, I'll put a bullet in my head. While I was in the SEALs I had to wait because we were in a war. Bill Shepherd—he's a very famous SEAL and my mentor—brought me here to the headquarters and taught me so much about Science & Technology. I am working S&T still as a consultant. So in the end I keep extending my life as a man, but I need to be done with that or come to some kind of a truce within myself.

Anne nodded taking notes again—she had to be serious from here on in—she'd agreed to be his biographer.

"So when does my life start?" Chris asked. "I have to start being myself."

Chris left Anne to drive to his mother's house and relax for the night.

BLOWBACK AT HOME—READING THE DALAI LAMA

Chris was staying over at his mother's home and was elated about the success of his speech. He came home and told his sister Karen and her husband, who now lived there, as well as a couple of their friends who had stopped by for beers about how he spoke right alongside the Deputy Assistant Secretary of Defense, a famous author, and was seated at the head table as their peers.

"How can you brief at the Pentagon knowing that you dress *like this* at home?" Chris's sister Karen asked. Disgust laced her voice and filled her face. She was nursing another glass of wine and already had drank a few too many.

"What would those top brass think if they knew?" Karen continued using a taunting voice.

"They're my colleagues! I work with them on a daily basis!" Chris retorted. "They respect me! As I respect them!"

"But what if they *knew* that you—an ex-Navy SEAL—are now at home wearing a dress! If you were a hairdresser, maybe your co-workers would accept it, but you're a Navy SEAL. It's not allowed for you!" Karen pressed on, repeating her old line.

"Listen, I'm tired, just leave me alone," Chris answered. None of his family accepted his female gender identity. But for now he was relaxing at home and had changed out of the male business clothes he still wore at work into his female clothes. He wanted to bask in his success, unwind and relax.

"I need to sleep," Chris announced as Karen and her husband refilled their drinks. He stood up from the table and retreated across the room to flop down on the couch—his bed for the night. Picking up his book—the latest from the Dalai Lama—he tried to tune them out. But Karen and her crowd weren't ready to retire yet and Karen wasn't giving up. She followed Chris to the couch and kept needling him.

"You're in *my house*," Karen said poking Chris in the chest. That was technically true. They had taken over the payments when they moved in. Deciding not to debate his drunk sister, Chris ignored her and continued to read from "Insights from the Dalai Lama".

Angered that he was tuning her out, Karen suddenly grabbed Chris by his shirt. "You need to listen to me! I am not done! You're in my house!" she shouted.

"I just want to sleep!" Chris answered rolling his eyes and laughing at her. "Leave me alone!"

Then perhaps more drunk than she realized and reverting to the immature behaviors of their childhood, Karen suddenly hauled off and punched Chris squarely in the mouth.

"Get the fuck out of *my* house!" she shouted.

"You hit me? *What are you doing?*" Chris shouted back, jumping to his feet. "If you want me to become a man, then I'll be a man; and if you hit me again, then you are stepping into man shoes and I'll smack the shit out of you!"

"What's going on in here?" Chris's mom shouted as she entered the room. "Get away from the angry SEAL!" she continued as she took in the scene—Chris standing ready to defend himself and Karen drunk and staggering back from him. As their mother ordered Karen protectively to move away, she turned to Chris with no understanding of what had just occurred and poured all her contempt out on him. "You need to stop drinking so much and get into anger management classes!"

"*Me? Seriously?* You are yelling at *me?*" Chris shouted back at their mother, astounded that she was accusing him.

"You need to leave!" their mother continued, waving her arm and pointing him to the door.

"Okay, I'm leaving," Chris answered. "I'm leaving forever."

"You saw it all!" Chris said turning to Chip, his brother-in-law, for support as Chris angrily gathered up his things. "You saw Karen come over and hit me! I was *reading* and you see *what book* I'm reading—it's the *Dalai Lama* for Christ's sake! I'm trying to chill out and bring peace to myself and she punched me while I was reading the *Dalai Lama!*"

Chip nodded but Chris could see that there was not going to be any support there and no changing his mother's opinion now that she had made up his mind that the fight was his fault, just like his younger years. Her arms were angrily crossed and her face was resolute. Chris picked up his things and left.

I'm not doing this anymore! I'm not and never was lying to anyone! That's bullshit! I'm me and have always been! Chris vowed to himself as he got in his car and drove angrily away from his family home. *Tomorrow*

I'm telling my co-workers. I'm going into work as a woman! As myself in my own clothes! I'm done! I'm not going to disguise anything anymore! My colleagues at the Pentagon will accept me. I'm good at what I do and they constantly seek me out for consultation and advice. Tomorrow, I'm out to everyone!

With no place to turn that late at night and also not wanting to drive around Maryland after drinking, Chris spent the night in his rental car a few miles away from his mother's house.

COMING OUT

The next night Anne arrived again after work to meet Chris at another bar in Crystal City where Pentagon workers frequented. Walking into the bar, Anne saw that Chris was dressed again in a tasteful work dress, black nylons and black boots. And there was crowd of people gathered at his table—all in work attire.

"Hi, I'm Clay Porter," one of the men said, coming to greet her. "I met you the other day at the lecture—but you don't remember," he explained and with her head spinning to catch up Anne suddenly understood, *These are his colleagues—he went to work "dressed up"!*

Indeed, fed up with his sister's assault, Chris had decided to show his entire office his real self—no more hiding. When Anne arrived, the group was splitting up and some were heading over to Ruth's Chris Steakhouse, in the same building as Chris's office. Once settled at Ruth's Chris ordering food and drinks, one of the waitresses came to take Chris's order.

"You don't recognize me, do you?" he asked her, smiling demurely.

"Oh my God! It's Chris!" the waitress screamed, looking him over and then ran to get the others. Chris and his work colleagues often gathered here after a long day's work, putting back beers and talking in loud male voices, and the waitresses all knew Chris as a man.

"Tell me your shoe size honey," the waitress cooed, completely accepting of the situation. "If we are the same size, I'll bring you some that I never wear."

This, it turned out, was a frequent female response to seeing Chris "dressed up". Women seemed to be complimented that a man wanted to enter their world—and that he needed some help to do so. And most were more than ready to hand out all kinds of advice and assistance. Perhaps they all felt a certain satisfaction in having the roles reversed—they had all the power.

"I am done being in this male persona. I want to live a new life. I'm erasing myself, disassembling the man and rebuilding a woman." Chris explained that night after everyone had left. "I have to have hormones soon! I can get them on the black market, but they are dangerous and I want to do it under a doctor's care. But at the VA they want me to wait a year! They said I have to have been going to work as a woman, as well as dressing at home, *for a whole year*! They don't understand what a big deal it is for me—as a Navy SEAL—to come out at work. I finally did it today! I don't know how this is going to turn out. So far a lot of the guys are taking it well."

On the one hand, Chris was elated that he had "come out" at work—but he was also worried how it was going to play out in his work life and within the SEAL community. His desperation and need to become authentic and congruent in his life had finally come to a head, and now that he'd done it he didn't ever want to turn back although he worried what the costs would turn out to be.

"I hate me! I hate this shell," Chris repeated. "I can't wait to be at the end of life—to no longer be male or female. My shell doesn't match my soul! I think I will be a better person if I can match up, relax and start liking myself outside and in."

"You think the soul has a gender?" Anne asked. "I think you are really talking about your gender identity matching your body," she suggested gently.

"No, we are just energies when we die," Chris conceded but continued, "All my years going out on deployments, I guess I was just trying to end it, hoping I wouldn't come back and have to deal with all of this."

***

That night when Anne offered to drop Chris at his hotel they walked together to Anne's car. Getting into the passenger side, Chris stretched out his long legs and primped while saying, "This is what I want, to ride on this side of the car, to have my mate over there and to be taken care of for once in my life."

The sadness in his voice, along with all he had already told her, made Anne realize that Chris had never really experienced that sense of love and being cared for that everyone in life longs for. And it seemed that he had early on in his life associated receiving nurture and avoiding abuse with physical beauty and being female. And now he believed as an adult that if he finally became a beautiful female perhaps he could finally be loved and cared for. That night Anne drove away from the hotel with a heavy heart, feeling his sadness and despair deep in her soul.

***

"I don't know if you heard about what's going on with me right now," Chris spoke over the phone to Shep the next day to explain his dramatic move.

"I heard a few things yesterday," Shep answered.

Shep meant the world to Chris and Chris was stumbling over his words, trying to find the right ones to tell his beloved mentor what was going on:

"You know I've been depressed and struggling with PTSD for awhile now and I have some other issues as well," Chris said and after a brief hesitation he spit it out, "I also have a gender identity disorder."

Shep paused in silence and then answered, concern lacing his voice, "Chris, you know I love you like a son! With all you've done for our country, your dozens of tours and all you've done for me, you do whatever you need to."

"Okay, thanks boss!" Chris answered, his voice breaking with emotion.

"Listen Chris, why don't you come in later this afternoon and we can talk things over as far as dealing with the rest of the organization," Shep suggested. Chris was one of his favorites, and he wasn't completely sure yet what Chris meant by his gender identity disorder or where he was headed.

"Uh, Shep," Chris answered hesitating a few seconds, "I can come in, but I'm wearing a dress. I'm dressed as a girl."

"Listen Chris, I don't care if you are wearing a clown suit!" Shep answered. "I care what's inside, your mind, your experience, you as a person—not what you are wearing," Shep continued. "And I want you to stay safe and take care of yourself. See you soon!"

Later that day, Shep smiled seeing Chris in a very demure yet elegant dress when they met outside the restaurant.

"Chris you look really good. You look happy!" Shep exclaimed. And pulling open the door Shep added with a half smile, "Ladies first!"

***

"Sir, I don't know if you've heard anything about what's going on with me," Chris began his next and perhaps most difficult call about his now-public situation to Glenn, his big boss at the Pentagon.

"Well I got a call from Bill Shepherd this afternoon saying that you'd be calling, but that's all I know," Glenn answered.

"Sir you know all that I've done, the deployments I've been on," Chris started. "I have PTSD and depression and some other issues," Chris began, laying the groundwork.

"Yes," Glenn answered, waiting for the rest.

"I also have some other issues," Chris continued, hesitating for a moment and then spit it out, "I have a gender identity disorder."

The line was silent for a moment and Chris felt his heart skip a beat.

"Is that all?" Glenn gruffly sputtered. "So you're *not* doing drugs, and you *didn't* killed anyone?" he asked half joking.

"No sir!" Chris answered.

"Oh, that's nothing!" the General replied. "You know I get all kinds of crazies up here. You're fine."

Both relieved and agreeing that's Chris's gender identity "disorder" was a nonissue, they finished their conversation and hung up the phone.

***

From that point on in his life, Chris now became Kristin or Kris. Her boss at the Pentagon still wanted Kris, just like Shep, for the experience, knowledge and ability—things that didn't change with gender. She was the happiest ever in her life. Her life as Kristin Beck had just begun.

A New Misfit

"It's beautiful!" Anne said as Kristin walked her through "The Misfit Mansion", a house built in the late 1800s. She had just flown in and would be staying the week with Kristin—making interviews and seeing Kris's life close up. Anne looked around the two-story, hundred year old stucco house: its curved archways separated the main entrance from the dining room and living room, one each side, and the many curved features worked into the front entrance, the porch and the roof along with the beautiful ornate wood-working, She understood why this house resonated: it was filled with curvy arches; it was feminine.

"Lovely," she said as she looked at the gleaming hardwood floors and many original pieces of furniture. SEAL's paraphernalia was also strewn throughout the house—photos, banners, and framed insignia hanging from the walls and over the fireplace mantel and arranged artfully behind the couches.

"The house is full right now, so I'm giving you my room," Kris said as she showed Anne upstairs. "I'll sleep downstairs on the couch."

The upstairs had three bedrooms, all with beautiful original wood windows on three sides of the house. The house was literally filled with bright shining light.

On Saturday morning Kris woke up at seven a.m. for a nine a.m. appointment with Karen, the owner and stylist at The Hair Hospital in St. Petersburg, and waited outside the door for fifteen minutes before the appointment.

"You can still do the extensions?" Kris asked anxiously when Karen arrived. "I remember you said maybe you wouldn't have time?"

"No, I have time darling," Karen answered, smiling warmly. "We'll get you all fixed up." For the next four hours Kristin sat in a sundress and wedge heels with her long legs extended over the chair as Karen dyed, glued and styled an entirely new look into Kris's medium length brown hair. When Kristin looked up after the final blowout she saw the person she always knew she was: a beautiful girl with a great full head of hair!

Arriving home, Kristin enjoyed the admiration of Anne and Amie and then the three walked the two short blocks to Sam's, a neighborhood restaurant where they ordered lunch and Bloody Marys on the deck. Meanwhile, Shep called and wanted to meet again—he'd looked into things and thought there was a bit more to discuss.

***

"Have a seat," Kris said, offering a chair and a Diet Coke to Shep and introducing him to Anne. "Anne's helping me write my biography," Kris explained.

Shep nodded and Kris continued suddenly smiling shyly at him. "So this is my new hair." Shep smiled without losing a beat. Clearly it would take a lot more than a dress, high heels and hair extensions to throw their relationship off kilter.

"So what do you think about all of this—how it's all going to go down?" Anne asked, interested to gauge what an insider expected to happen for Kris in her work world.

"Kris is still the same person," Shep answered, smiling wryly. "He hasn't lost his or her skill set. Kris is still one of us. This is a *personal* choice—the professional is still there. But there will be some challenges."

"The SEAL network is buzzing, that's for sure," Shep added, turning to Kris. "Most of it's been fine, but there was one highly upset caller—someone you know well. I'm not going to tell you who but we had a long argument and I finally ended by telling him, 'You know the tours Kris has been on for this country. You have to accept that Kris is a *human being*—that comes with the territory!'"

"So *some* were upset?" Kris repeated, steeling herself for tough news.

"Yes, there were quite a few calls, but *only one* who was really upset. Everyone else is taking it fine, as far as I can tell," Shep reassured Kris.

"Yeah, I suppose a lot of them are saying 'What the fuck?' some of the others are saying 'Whatever' and a few of them are saying 'Right on!'" Kris commented.

"You can't do anything in this community that some won't approve of—there will always be a few..." Shep reassured. Then turning to Anne he explained, "A lot of people are jealous of Kris. He's done a lot of things. He's creative and they're not. He creates a lot of influence with government circles and they may be thinking, *Who the hell is this guy?*

"I came over today to talk to you about all that's got to be done. With all the SEALs buzzing about this, there's bound to be public exposure. You have to be ready. I won't be surprised if some agent comes and asks if you can do public speaking, offers you a contract. You have to prepare on a number of levels—for you, your family and for the SEALs. You need to write a press release," Shep finished.

"Okay, we can do that," Kris nodded, taking in the import of what Shep was saying.

"What do you think it should say?" Anne asked.

"Tell it raw—say what it is," Shep answered. "What's going on, the background—who Kris is, her position, how this come about, and what's next?

"You also need to go over and talk to the Wounded Warrior and Care Coalition [at SOCOM]," Shep advised. "You might want to ask them about getting a lawyer to help with all of these issues."

Kris reflected on how SOCOM had been working hard to set up support networks for the guys coming home and were really going the extra mile. SOCOM lives by the "SOF Truths", one of them being "Humans are more important than hardware."

"What about this book and clearance issues? Don't we need to get that vetted by SOCOM?" Anne asked.

"Yes, Kris has special clearances," Shep explained, not realizing that Anne, as the wife of a U.S. Ambassador, was aware of—and had carried herself—high-level clearances. "He's been in positions of unique trust. It's important that this is framed correctly—that he's disclosed things correctly over the years in his polygraphs and that he hasn't deceived anyone. There are issues of being seen as susceptible to bribery or compromise." Then turning to Kris he added, "You need to get the security guys involved."

"Kris served under *Don't Ask/Don't Tell*," Anne pointed out. "He followed official military policy of the times. How can anyone fault him for that?"

"I always answered that question on the [security clearance] polygraph, 'No, there is nothing in my life that I can be blackmailed for,' because there was nothing," Kris added. "I would have said, 'Go ahead and tell!' if anyone threatened me! Of course I wanted my own timing, but I would have been loyal to my country of course."

"You need to give this press release to the guys at SOCOM and let them vet it," Shep advised. "Tell them something like, 'I'm prepared to respond to anyone, including the media, and I want your counsel before I do this. I'm giving you this draft press statement to let me know if there is anything inappropriate in it.' And you should ask, 'Do you have any guidelines for me in speaking to the media?'

"You should also ask for one or two weeks of administrative leave," Shep continued. "The security guys may want to do a retrospective analysis to review your situation, but in the end they will make a written statement and your security status will be unaffected."

Shep also suggested Kris be evaluated by the CARE Coalition.

"You know there's two kinds of insanity," Shep said, turning to Anne. "There's the camp where the person thinks I'm to blame—something is wrong with me. And then there's the camp that believes the world is out of order—it's not me."

Anne nodded wondering, *Which is it for Kris? She's gone both ways on that one!*

Kris had probably spent the majority of her life blaming herself for the mismatch in gender identity and actual body—so much so that she lived in a near constant state of being almost suicidal. Now perhaps she had come to the opposite view, believing that she needed to find congruency and live authentically and that the only viable way to do that was to take hormones and change her body surgically to match her gender identity.

"Remember even when I was working for you boss, I was living so far out of the box," Kris said, reminding Shep about her presentation at the conference at the Pentagon on cyber warfare. "No matter what I've been on the outside, I'm a weird SEAL and I embrace my weirdness," Kris continued smiling brightly. "I think my life—that I also have a female side—has made me much more than just what BUD/S makes you. I'm not just a shooter and a door-kicker. I can probably think about irregular and unconventional warfare, innovation and many things much more creatively than any other SEAL team member can! I have a perspective and points of view that most military or government officials will never have."

As Shep got up to leave, he glanced over his shoulder toward the driveway. "If you want my bet," he said, "I'll wager one night's dinner, in a restaurant, that you'll have news trucks parked outside this house within the week. I bet they'll be here by next weekend—by next Friday night."

I better hurry and type that press release! Anne thought looking at Kris. She could see how deeply her emotions were engaged in all that was suddenly happening, and despite her adult stature and years of experience operating in a responsible capacity, Anne could also see that Kris seemed a bit like a vulnerable adolescent girl, caught up in the fun of having new equipment and new dresses to hang on the equipment. It would be good to lend a helping hand.

THE T-GIRLS

Teri, a long-time friend who often organized the transgender friends to get together and go out as "girls," had called and let Kris know she was trying to pull a group of T-girls (Transgender Girls) together to meet at Flamingos, a GLBT resort, and later carry on to Georgie's, a gay bar where Kris enjoyed seeing his favorite bartender DJ. Both were places where the T-girls found refuge away from the 'public' who sometimes could be mean.

Super excited about the new hair extensions, Kris picked out a short black-and-white skull-printed party dress that had wide straps on the top, and close fitting bodice and flared out from the waist down.

Anne helped Kris put electric rollers in her new hair and style it. Kris put her make up on, showing Anne how she carefully covered what was left of her beard after the laser treatments and how she used white and darker powders to contour her nose and cheeks.

She's quite a make-up artist! Anne thought to herself smiling, and she offered her one of the necklaces her daughter had hand designed in black acrylic to complete the outfit.

Arriving first at the club Anne wondered briefly, "Is it okay for me to be here? Does anyone mind?"

"Are you kidding? Everyone is invited to Gay Bars. That's what 'Diversity' means. There are a lot of single GGs (Genetic Girls) that come here to dance; they feel safe," Kris said and Anne felt good about the acceptance. It was funny to be on the other side of it.

Kris and Anne passed through to an outer courtyard where there was a giant lit-up pool surrounded by creatively lit palm trees. The lights combined with the water made a stunning navy blue and gold glow.

"Can we eat out here?" Anne asked glad to be out in the balmy Florida air under the moonlight.

Kris and Anne ordered crab cakes along with glasses of wine and settled in chat.

"You know I come here to have some peace in my soul," Kris said looking around their surroundings. "I feel so liberated now that I've come out. I am really starting to like myself now; I really feel alive and happy."

Anne nodded listening.

"I want to be happy," Kris continued. "If this makes me happy, can that be okay with all the rednecks and bigots out there? I was fighting for the last two years for my life—feeling suicidal at times. Does that count for anything?"

Anne thought that Kris sounded suicidal her whole adult life: the way he as a SEAL kept going back into war, trying to leave his life insurance for his boys. But Kris's sentiment was right on. *It isn't her fault how her mind and identity were shaped—whether it be from DNA, chemicals in our environmental, or early childhood. Her responses to trauma, family dynamics and all the things that shape an identity were not choices, but things done to her,* Anne reflected. *And he had struggled so hard, for so many years to overcome it—marrying and divorcing twice and all the ruin that went with that.*

Kris could try a long course of psychotherapy to unearth the early formations of her gender identity and try to redo it, but it is highly doubtful that such psychotherapy would work, since there are many indications that once-formed, gender identities are unlikely to ever change. Existing standards of care, in fact, recommend that individuals with significant discomfort with the match between their gender identity and body after a careful clinical assessment should be therapeutically supported to consider and if desired, move through three additional elements or phases of therapy—to address their distress. These include: having a real-life experience in the desired role, taking hormones of the desired gender, and surgery to change the genitalia and other sex characteristics. Not all individuals suffering from gender dysphoria will want or need all three elements and they may order the phases according to their individual needs and desires. And some will find that they do not need or want to take any action to change their bodies—finding inner peace in their own unique ways. Treatments of this sort generally have positive outcomes in terms of improved function, self-esteem, reduced anxiety and sense of well being. At least with hormones and surgery Kris would have a known outcome: her body would come to match her inner gender identity.

She could also try to come to peace with the mismatch—realizing that gender is a culturally-constructed concept in any case—but this too would take a great deal of emotional work to accept both her inner sense of self and outer body in a mismatched state of being.

Who is to say what the right course of action should be and if there is even a "right course" in gender identity cases. Through a confluence of forces—many that we even today do not fully understand—Kris had been deeply set off course from the current society's sense of "normal" development in which body and gender identity match, and it wasn't fair that others blamed her for that or claimed that it was her responsibility to fix—especially when she lacked the tools to do so.

"The rednecks, Christians and bigots would say, 'You don't deserve to live!'" Kris said with sadness filling her eyes as both sat silently for a moment taking that level of hate onboard.

"I think I deserve to live! And to be happy?" Kris rebutted angrily and again reverted back to the pain, "Please, I do deserve to live!"

Anne nodded, letting Kris run the course of her pain, knowing she needed to get it out.

"I try to be a human as a female, but people point at me and laugh," Kris continued. "They snicker and act like I don't deserve anything. They think I don't deserve respect—they laugh. They don't even know me," Kris paused for a bit then continued. "Can I have some freedom? Can I be an American? I don't deserve the disrespect and ridicule they throw at me! People don't point at wheelchairs and laugh. But they laugh at me! I feel like Quasimodo! I feel extremely sorry for kids growing up with this issue—girls and boys. The suicide rate among transgender kids is off the charts—it's above fifty percent! It's a shame and I want to reach out to all of them. They shouldn't be bullied; they are people and deserve happiness."

Anne nodded again and kept listening.

"Life, liberty and the pursuit of happiness," Kris said. "I fought for the first two—can I have the third?" Kris asked, referring to the inalienable rights that all human beings are endowed with—for the protection of which they institute governments. "I am going to start a blog—maybe I will be able to help a few of the younger kids out there with gender issues. I want to go to high schools and give talks; I am a sheepdog after all. I can keep the wolves at bay."

"To happiness," Anne answered raising her glass and together they toasted Kris's future.

Teri arrived soon after. Looking up from her meal, Anne saw first the long and shapely white tights-clad legs, then the short skirt and then the long lashes and sparkling eyes looking demurely from under a cute pixie cut wig.

"Hi!" Anne said, not sure how the night would play out and how exactly to relate to Teri—should she put her notebook and pen away? But in no time Teri was opening up about what it was like to be a T-girl and about the relationship she shared with Kris.

"At first I would go to hotels and dress up," Teri explained, "and I would always run out the door for just a few seconds, down the hallway past one or two doors and then eventually all the way down the hall."

Anne nodded, glad to be trusted and interested to learn more.

"If all you do is go to a hotel room and dress up, it's never enough. I'd go down five rooms and go back, then I'd go ten rooms and back and then sometimes I'd get caught. Dressing in a room wasn't enough of a fulfillment for me. I wanted to go out and show myself."

"Did you always feel you were a woman?" Anne asked wondering what Teri's story would be.

"I dated women for twenty years," Teri answered, suddenly sounding and looking masculine again. It was interesting for Anne to see how Teri changed the entire musculature of her face when taking the perspective of one gender identity or the other. As Teri continued, her face reverted back to a feminine look, "I debuted in '98 at a fetish party. I got the courage there to come out. People told me, 'Wow you look great!'"

"Did you dress when you were younger too?" Anne asked, curious about how Teri developed her female gender identity.

"Yes, I'd take my sister and mother's stuff," Teri explained. "Once I took these really beautiful wedge shoes of my sisters—they were orangey reddish—and I wore them around in my room. But I have bigger feet than my sister so when I put them back and she put them on for church the next day she was surprised and said, 'Wow my shoes feel stretched!'" Teri laughedmischievously.

"I learned so much tradecraft—how to hide things!" Kris volunteered,also laughing. "I don't do drag queen looks, but it is fun to do drag. I learned a lot from the drag queens about make up; Cherri Poppins taught me makeup. But I just want to be a nice girl from down the street."

"It's stupid to wear foam to make a big bootie or hips," Teri noted. "A man feels that right away and knows it's not you—that it's just foam. I'd like to be [a girl] full-time," she added her face suddenly turning sad.

"Samantha used to come here with us all dressed," Kris recalled as the conversation veered onto other topics. "She accepted me at first. She would come out with us all the time!"

"That's the bait," Teri answered knowingly. "Then they reel you in and try to change you."

"She thought she could cure me," Kris added and both nodded—Teri obviously had lived through something similar.

Soon Allison, another T-girl, joined. It was Allison's first night to join the group and she was a bit unsure of the make-up and hair routine. Looking at Allison, Anne saw a big-nosed, large-framed man in a dress—who was also a very lovely bigger woman with an infectious smile that caused her face to light up and a dimple to appear on one cheek. It was totally confusing to Anne.

Teri, as the person who many of the T-girls turned to when first coming out, took Allison off to the bar to talk quietly together while Kris and Anne finished their meal and settled up their bill.

No More Disguises

"This is one of the disguises I ran around the world in for many years," Kris wrote the next afternoon, updating her LinkedIn photo by putting up a bearded Taliban-looking picture of herself from the days in Afghanistan. "Soon I'll be taking off all the disguises," she cryptically added.

***

"You want to go shopping?" Kris asked Anne. "Most of my clothes are for hanging around the house or going out dancing. I need to buy a professional wardrobe for work."

"Sure," Anne answered.

The first stop was to a women's clothing store. Kris quickly picked an array of blouses, pants, skirts and blazers—all sophisticated professional attire, taste acquired from Kris's sisters—to take into the dressing room. Anne sat on a bench waiting to see each outfit and commented and exchanged sizes when they weren't right. Soon black, blue, and red blazers were chosen, a black and blue skirt, four blouses and three pairs of ladies' pants. Then the two pressed onwards to the shoe store.

Making for the clearance rack first given how much had been spent at the first store, Kris quickly selected some medium-heeled, stylish ladies' shoes. Then the two browsed over the full price racks adding a few more selections. Soon Kris was at the checkout paying for all the purchases. "I don't think I've ever been in either of these two stores and bought nothing!" Anne remarked, thinking the support role had drained her of any inclination to shop.

Back at home, Kris piled the clothes on the bed and gave Amie a "fashion show" trying the outfits on one by one.

"I love them all but the red blazer," Amie commented as she lay back on the bed watching the "show". "It doesn't fit your shoulders right honey, but I think you can get it altered and then it will be perfect. It's a great color for you!"

Selecting one of the outfits, Kris dressed in a black skirt, black-and-white striped knit blouse and black blazer and sleek black heels and then reappeared in the living room asking Anne, "Ready to head out?"

"I can't believe Pete leaves me with no gas in my truck!" Kris commented when they got back in her truck to go to Lieutenant Colonel Borjes' house. "Whenever I'm in Washington, D.C. he takes my truck and always when I come home it's on empty!"

"He helps you at home in return for not paying rent?" Anne asked not wanting to comment much on whatever agreement they had worked out.

"Yes, kind of, but he let a lot of the plants die while I was gone and now the toilet and the sink are broken!" Kris exclaimed.

"You think maybe you need to tighten up your boundaries a bit?" Anne gently asked.

"I have no boundaries, remember," Kris exclaimed angrily, "It goes like this: a regular human being accepts me and I hold out my hand to him and say, 'Take all my money!'" She angrily threw her open hand out to demonstrate, and continued, "You like me? Let me give you all I have!"

A sad silence filled the air between them until Anne commented, "Kris maybe now that you are getting yourself into an authentic place where your gender identity and your body match, you won't have to lie anymore about how you are feeling. Maybe as you come to love and acceptance of yourself and find that with others. Not everybody will accept it—but as you find real love and real acceptance, you won't feel the need to do that anymore?"

"Yeah, I hope so," Kris answered sadly.

Making New Adjustments in Old Relationships

"Hello, come on in!" Christy Borjes said, ushering Anne and Kris into the kitchen of the Borjes home.

"So this is the new you?" Christy asked, looking at Kris with a warm and accepting smile on her face. Christy was a professional photographer and the wife of a good friend. Kris had asked if she could stop by to discuss if Christy might take a few professional photos for her—in case it all broke in the press.

"I'd like to be ready to have a good photo to put forward," Kris explained, "And if you want, I'd love for you to make the back photo cover for the book too." "I'm going to put a picture of me as a bearded SEAL on the front cover," she added laughing.

"If you want, we can take one right now—for you to be ready," Christy answered. "But for the real ones you should come when I have more time—maybe on Tuesday night? Come for dinner and we'll take photos after that."

Kris smiled and followed Christy down the hall to her home studio where Christy set up lights and posed Kris in front of a large professional photographer's screen.

"Maybe we should use the flag too?" Kris prompted and everyone agreed it was a good idea. Soon Colonel Borjes—Karl—arrived and hung it behind Kris on the screen.

After getting some good shots, the group made their way back to the kitchen—evidently the heart of the Borjes home and talked for a little while.

"It's hard for me," Karl admitted. "It's terrible to say, but I've got to be honest. I knew you as a man and this is not easy to take in!"

Then turning to Anne, Karl continued, "We love Chris. He's a part of our family and always will be!"

SOUND BYTES

"Tomorrow we'll go to see the CARE coalition over at SOCOM," Kris explained to Anne as he flipped on the switch to the salt-water aquarium, illuminating the blue, gold, orange and yellow fish and tiny brown lobster crabs swimming inside. Pete stood behind the bar while Amie and Anne pulled up seats on the lawn chairs to watch the fish. Amie poured out some red wine. Kris walked back into the house to get some papers.

"Listen guys, if it's really true that this place could be surrounded by news trucks next week maybe you should all be practicing your sound bytes?" Anne suggested. "You want to practice?" She picked up a pen from the bar and turned to Aime.

"So tell us miss, you live in this house with Kris Beck?" Anne asked, "What is your relationship to her? Can you give us a comment?"

"Kris is a real hero and fought for her country," Amie answered without losing a beat. "She's also a very good person."

"Are you his lover?" Anne continued playing the newscaster with a sly smile crossing her face.

"No! We are just friends," Amie answered confidently.

"And you sir, you live in this house as well?" Anne said turning the fake microphone on Pete. He nodded and Anne continued, "Are the *two of you* lovers?'

"I think I'm going to punch them out," Pete answered shaking his head with disgust.

"No, Petey, you can't punch them!" Amie laughed. "You have to have an answer ready!"

"Okay I know what I'll say," Pete answered, turning back to Anne and waiting for her to repeat the question while he readied himself to make a serious statement. She repeated the question holding the fake microphone in his face and Pete answered in complete seriousness with no smile or laughter accompanying his statement, "No, I'm not his lover. I don't happen to roll that way. I love to suck titties and lick pussy!"

Amie erupted in shocked laughter and screamed, "Oh Petey! You can't say *that*!"

"You better stay away from the press." Anne laughed and removed the microphone while Petey flipped open a beer, shaking his head. When Kris returned, Amie repeated Pete's statement while convulsing in laughter.

"No press for you my boy," Kris agreed.

Telling SOCOM

"You're looking good!" Anne remarked as Kris appeared the next morning wearing her new black striped knit blouse and black skirt. Her long, slim legs went on forever, accentuated by high heels.

"This is the first time in my life that I am truly happy," Kris said as the two piled into her to meet the contractor Kris had on the schedule to meet to talk about a mini-submarine.

When they arrived to the contractor's office Kris discussed the project with them while Anne watched. It didn't seem to bother anybody that Kris had shown up dressed as a woman and at one point she explained to them, "I know this might be a little strange for you—but I have a gender identity thing and I'm in the middle of a change." They nodded and things seemed to be cool.

Meanwhile Anne watched while the former SEAL—Kristin Beck—explained the operator's need, the technology and the vision for the project. She knew her stuff and they listened raptly—never missing a beat over the woman who was addressing them. Indeed it was a very innovative project and just one of many combat useful inventions that Kris had been part of.

That night Kris put up a new photo to her LinkedIn profile—the one taken by Christy of Kris standing in front of the American flag. This time Kris wrote, "I am now taking off all my disguises and letting the world know my true identity as a woman." Kris also changed her name on her profile page to Kristin Beck.

Inside Kris had wondered for a very long time if her family had already rejected her for wanting to live out her gender identity as a female, how would the SEALs respond? Kris imagined some of them saying, *I want to kill you!* Inside she felt a deep hurt as she mused over her fears of total rejection. *We were so close—brothers really,* Kris wondered sadly. *Why can't they accept me as I really am?*

Soon, the responses from SEALs stationed all around the world suddenly started pouring in:

"Brother, I am with you…being a SEAL is hard, This looks harder. Peace."

"I can't say I understand the decision but I respect the courage. Peace and happiness be upon you... Jim"

***

"Kris, I just recently heard the news regarding your announcement. I just wanted to drop you a note and tell you that Kris has all the support and respect from me that Chris had...and quite possibly more. While I'm definitely surprised, I'm also in amazement at the strength you possess and the courage necessary to combat the strangers and "friends" that I'm guessing have reared their ugly heads prior to and since your announcement. Congratulations and please remember that you were, are, and always will be a good friend and welcome as a friend at home. Let me or anyone here know if you need anything. v/r, Kyle"

***

"Hey, I don't give a rat's ass what you do, I'll support you all the way with anything in your life, Kris. ... Life is too short to live a lie. Tony"

***

"Hey Chris, WOW...well I don't know what to say. I can't tell if this is an elaborate "Team-Guy" hoax or if it's on the level?. . . Either way I think you should know my thoughts…:

1. I don't give a damn if you are a man or a woman, purple, black, Asian, tall, short, fat, skinny, etc. . . . . You're a Team Guy first and foremost and you always will be.

2. I'll drink a beer with you anytime, anywhere, for any reason, no matter how you are dressed...especially if you're buying!

3. You're right, I am from Northern Cali . . . and my father taught me when I was way young: "There are plenty of great reasons to hate a person. The color of a person's skin, who he/she dates/marries, and how much money they have or don't have are just not good reasons..." I live by this advice and my Dad was right, cause I hate a whole ton of people just not for bullshit reasons.

Anyway if it's a joke, then it was amazingly well done but in bad taste based on my understanding of the difficulty the transgendered have in being accepted (see, I am from SF!) and for the current climate. If it's true then, I wish you all the best, I will still call you brother or sister, whichever you prefer, and let me know when you wanna buy me a couple of beers . . . although I may need a shot a whiskey as well! Take care and I hope to hear from you soon. Rich"

***

"Kris - Your recent announcement is a lot for me to wrap my mind around. I am encouraged by the number of supportive messages that I've seen from Brother Rats. . . . At the end of the day, I say live and let live . . . Take care and Semper Fi! Drew"

"Chris, Let me begin with the statement that I would like you to read my words as authentic and not as some cut and paste, disingenuous, politically correct press statement. I am thankful that your decision was to confront your challenges rather than, as you stated in your own words, "put a shotgun in your mouth". I further appreciate your honesty in stating that gender identity has been a struggle since grade school. That allows all of us to move on from the easy response of "Chris has significant PTSD issues".... Your oath and your defense of our constitution and the principles it calls us to aspire to deserve my respect and my honesty. Those principles and that document are (and I do not use this next word lightly at all) sacred to those of us on this message thread. Every adult US citizen 'rates' to choose their own lifestyle and values. You have clearly made a specific, outside the box choice. A choice that I will defend regardless of my personal values ... May you find ease and lasting peace. Count on me to put you in my prayers. Scott"

***

"Kristin, You have brought the right stuff to many places and to all who know you. I personally find my life is much fuller because you have been my friend for over a decade.... My family and I are here for you anytime, anywhere. Time for you to be happy. You do me honor being associated with you and calling you my friend. Fair winds, I will there when you need me. David"

Nearly twenty SEALs responded—sending their concern and love, with a few making religious statements and asking questions as to whether it was a good course of action, but in the main most seemed to understand and accept her decision. Kristin was very comforted to see their responses.

And when Anne texted the news to Todd Veazie, a SEAL friend posted to the White House to oversee the Michelle Obama's Joining Forces initiative, Todd texted back:

"Please give her my best regards and full support ... I hope Chris finds peace in this storm. He is one of the really good ones. It's great to know that Shep has his back. Count me in that group."

It wasn't only the SEALs who were responding. Some of the guys that Kris had trained and worked with were also stopping by—many because the relationships were still strong and the projects they were jointly pursuing were active. John, a former submariner whom Kris had contacted to discuss a mini-submarine project, stopped by.

"So what do you think?" Anne asked John when he saw Kris for the first time, dressed for work in a navy blue skirt with a white and blue sleeveless blouse and tall navy heels.

"At first I thought it's a joke. Like ha ha, it's a joke!" John answered. "And I couldn't make up my mind if you were mind fucking me or not."

Kris pulled up lawn chairs on the patio to sit and offered beers.

"I will support you," John said, lifting his beer to Kris. "You paid your dues and five other guys dues as well! I know the shit you guys went through."

John went on to talk about his time in the submarines, when the military policy of Don't Ask/Don't Tell first came out and the resistance to allowing women to serve on subs—which he attributed far more to the Submariners Wives' Association than to the military itself—and his views on women becoming SEALs.

"I think some women can make it through the training," John offered. "It's a combination of mental and physical anguish—but it can't be watered down for the women, and they have to go through the hazing the same as the men because it's there for a purpose, to make sure that later they won't mentally break. If they can do that, they can be SEALs.

"The SEALs respected me, and Kris's respect towards me, means the world to me," John concluded and then returned to Kris's "coming out". "I'm in full support. Did it shock the living shit out of me? Yes."

"You know there are so many pros and cons about coming out," Kris piped in. "And I wouldn't wish this on anyone. It would be so much easier to not have this issue."

"Yes passing this may be worse than passing BUD/S," John commented. "Here's what the problem is going to be. Some of them are not secure in their masculinity. Me—I don't give a shit. If the shit hits the fan, I can take care of me and my family. To a lot of people that is what is considered masculine. That Kris decided to become a woman goes against all of that. And some are going to talk shit against her. But if it's not hurting anyone else who gives a flying fuck? It doesn't matter if you take two years transitioning or one week. You are still basically the same person. You still have all the skills and all the knowledge you had before."

PTSD on the Road

"I was always the GMV (Ground Mobility Vehicle) driver," Kris said as she drove with Anne to the Veteran's Administration (VA) in her black Ford pickup truck. A car in front of her slowed down for no reason, almost stopping.

"When they make you slow down, that's when they hit you!" Kris said irritably trying to fire her truck past the gridlock. She was referring to the rocket-propelled grenade launchers and the remotely-fired roadside IEDs that the enemy used to blow up American military vehicles in Iraq and Afghanistan.

"We would drive so frickin fast!" Kris continued, gunning her truck out of the slowed traffic—freeing them from imagined danger. "It felt like we could outdrive the explosion, but of course we couldn't—if it went off we'd all be killed."

"There was one particularly bad stretch," Kris continued, "We called it IED alley. We took a bunch of hits in that area in 2003."

"I talked to a soldier just the other night," Anne reflected. "He told me he can't drive off the base in North Carolina where he's stationed—he's got such bad PTSD from the IED attacks in Iraq that he now feels like he's driving outside the wire [into the Red Zone]." She didn't want to hit Kris with direct questions right now while she was driving who knows where: here or *over there*. Often she found that if she told other people's stories that had a commonality with the person's trauma, it helped them to open up about how it was for them.

"He singled me out at a military conference banquet dinner and talked to me for two hours about his PTSD. They were only giving him medication for it, no treatment and he's not doing well," Anne continued. "I drove him back to his hotel and since I don't remember Washington, D.C. so well—we've been overseas for thirteen years—I got lost for about an hour but I didn't care, because he need to talk. He almost jumped out of his skin for every intersection, every approaching car and when a bike whizzed by us I thought he'd have a heart attack!

"And he told me that he was eighteen years and six months in for his military service but might have to go out on one more deployment—even with that bad of PTSD—or be designated undeployable, which means he could lose his entire pension. It didn't seem right to me."

"You know that no one in the TEAMS says they have PTSD," Kris answered cynically. "They don't want to talk about it. You can't go on the missions if you're messed up, so everyone just bottles it up inside."

Anne nodded listening.

"We are all very good at covering up," Kris continued. "It was only after I retired and when I started talking to Kiki, my VA social worker that I started dumping out my emotions—regurgitating. She had to tell me 'Whoa! Slow down a bit, I can't keep up!'"

"How did you deal with your PTSD before that?" Anne asked.

"Beer, motorcycles, more beer." Kris answered nonchalantly. "You see how we drive?" Kris pointed out that she uses both feet: one on the accelerator, one on the brake—always ready to put the car in a spin.

"We drive with our arms down, thumbs out," Kris explained. "That way if you need to wipe the car and it spins the [steering] wheel, you don't break your thumbs off. And I keep my hands and arms down; that way if the airbag goes off I won't get my hands back in my face—although we didn't have airbags over there."

Glancing down at her right knee, Kris seemed to see the set-up of her former military vehicles in her mind's eye. "My pistol is always here." she explained, "so I can grab it and start shooting, but then there is that one story where Joey had his pistol under his leg and during a short stop it flew out onto the floor and then made its way under his seat. A firefight broke out and he couldn't find his pistol. Lesson learned was always have a holster or tuck it tight between the seat and the center console. I used to add Velcro to the sides of my pistol and grenades and stick it to my body armor and to the rug in the car."

Kris seemed to come back to the present.

"I hate driving in America!" She exclaimed as yet another car pulled in front and then slowed down, blocking the traffic's flow. "I wish someone would drive for me!"

To Anne's ears it sounds like the childhood wish repeated—the wish in the face of what feels like danger and life threat—to be a girl, to be loved and protected, instead of the boy who has to take care of it all. And this of course was now years later, layered over by twenty years of traumatic combat experiences in the SEALs.

VA & Care Coalition

"I'm here to see Kiki," Kris explained when they arrived at the Veteran's Administration treatment center. "I missed my appointment yesterday."

In a few short minutes they were ushered into Kiki's office. "She's with me," Kris said indicating that she was giving permission for Anne to be present.

"It's your health data," the short-cropped hair and elfin smiling Kiki said as she told them to sit down and pulled out her keyboard for note taking.

"I'm super, super happy. My PTSD is gone, I have no more depression, I don't need any more help," Kris explained as the two discussed that Kris had suddenly taken the step to "come out" at work.

"Yeah, you really sped things up!" Kiki reflected. "I remember you said you were going to do things slowly, open the green house and gardens (HealingGrounds.org) and maybe 'come out' in a few years after you got the Foundation going."

"I had to do it," Kris explained. "I was up in D.C. and my sister and I got in an argument—I am just tired of hiding and lying to myself. I want to like myself and really start to live. I like what RuPaul says: "How can you love anyone else, if you don't love yourself?"

"The tension can really build up right before," Kiki reflected. "It can feel like a giant explosion building up—ready to go off."

"Well I 'came out' last week at work," Kris said.

"And how did it go?" Kiki asked.

"Good! Everyone was cool. My mentor Bill Shepherd told me it didn't matter if I showed up in a clown suit—that he loves me like a son! Everyone else was fine," Kris said. "I think my PTSD is all cleared up. That's my story and I'm sticking to it." Kris smiled.

Anne listened with clinician ears, thinking this is the elation of sudden freedom from her gender constraints and feelings that she had to continue to be a man, but PTSD doesn't clear that way. Depression, maybe. *There's going to be some more serious ups and downs,* Anne thought to herself but kept silent.

"So I have an e-mail here that they've made a primary doctor switch for you," Kiki explained. "This doctor is an expert in hormone therapy."

"You mean I don't have to wait anymore?" Kris asked, bubbling over with joy.

"You'll have to ask her," Kiki answered, "but probably not."

"There are so many issues to fix! I'm going to get a new drivers license—I'm a female!" Kris continued determinedly. "Just going to the bathroom is an issue. I can get beat up going to the men's room in a dress, but until I start the hormones and really look female it's a serious issue using the ladies room! I want my driver's license to say I'm a female now—so I can prove it if anyone challenges me about which bathroom I'm using."

Kris wrapped up the short appointment, thanking Kiki for taking the time and as they departed Anne handed Kiki her business card and mentioned, "It's been really nice reading the responses on LinkedIn—a lot of support and statements about Kris being a hero no matter what her gender is. No one's been mean yet."

Kiki flashed a big smile cynically adding, "There's always time!"

As they walked down the hallway of the VA treatment center, Kris pointed at a large room. "That's the group therapy that I hate," Kris said.

Anne glanced into the doorway noticing some older guys seated in plastic chairs as she and Kris walked briskly down the hall to the exit.

"All they talk about is how when they came home from Vietnam they were called 'baby killers' and people were spitting on them," Kris sputtered. "Most of them are lying about their experiences—they probably saw it in a movie! I don't want to be in their bull sessions!"

"They may be hooking their pain to acceptable stories—stories that express their pain," Anne commented after a thoughtful silence. "Their pain is probably real even if the stories aren't."

WALKING THE GAUNTLET

"Fifty-one!" The tired looking woman at the VA optical clinic called out. Kris held the number fifty-six in her manicured hand.

"This VA seems really nice," Anne commented looking around, taking in the tall shiny glass windows, green plants and everything looking new and well cared for.

"Yeah, the ones in Tampa are great. We have the big commands here— a lot of Generals and Admirals, so they have to be extra good. Take a look around you; there are so many retired old guys, they really have to work extra. Florida—it's God's waiting room," Kris cracked and Anne burst into laughter.

"Navy SEAL who shot Osama bin Laden gives an interview," the television announced behind them and both Anne and Kris turned to see the news. The older Vietnam vets continued talking loudly over the breaking news feed, making it hard to hear.

"You might want to listen—this is *today's war!*" Kris commented, raising her voice enough to interrupt them. The old guys noticed the agitation in Kris's voice but didn't seem to register that though she was wearing nicely styled hair and a dress, she was in the body of a rather tall man and that she was demanding some respect for the guys in the war to which she'd given the last ten years of her life. Ignoring all but the anger—which seemed to register as faint alarm on their elderly faces, they continued droning on, not hearing Kris or the television. Kris repeated her comment, raising her voice.

"Let's move seats," Anne suggested, alarmed that a very ridiculous looking fight could break out between an ex Navy SEAL in a dress and some elderly Vietnam veterans. "I don't think these guys are hearing *anything!*" she added trying to make Kris see the absurdity of the situation.

"They only care about *their war and nothing else!*" Kris spat out as the two drew closer to the television. The story was already ending—something about the SEAL shooter now fearing for the lives of his young family. He was also struggling, having stepped down from the military due to the stress of his job and cumulative injuries—both mental and physical— but with no pension after a sixteen-year career in the SEALs.

The commentator explained the official military policy of not extending retirement for those serving less than twenty years and finished with a snide comment that the shooter had *volunteered* for his time in the Navy SEALs anyway.

"What the hell does that mean?" Anne asked—her turn to be irritated. "What does *volunteering* for the SEALs teams mean in terms of what he's suffering now? It's not like he signed up for PTSD and the inability to finish up his career to win a full retirement!"

"Yeah, it is his fault in a way. I am all busted up from the job; we all volunteered for the SEALs. Use us up and spit us out," Kris commented bitterly. "If he'd just taken a regular job on some ship in the Navy, he'd be fine now and able to put in his twenty years easy. He'd be getting full retirement instead of having killed Osama bin Laden and afraid for this family and his future now! Isn't it funny how in normal society "it's always someone else's fault," but when it comes to the military they stick the blame directly on our shoulders and then burn us to the ground."

"You think they could hunt him down here in the States?" Anne asked horrified at the thought.

"Yes. These are *terrorists! They kill women and children everyday!*" Kris answered. "Why wouldn't they? They've got sleeper cells everywhere. They deal in drugs, kidnapping and slavery around the world to raise money for their terrorist crimes. He's right to be concerned. I can't imagine what he went through when he got back stateside—not to mention what his family is dealing with now."

Anne nodded imagining how awful that would be—to have chased and fought terrorists for the past ten years and then to live with an awareness that one—or worse yet, one's wife and little children—could be hunted down and killed—anytime, anywhere.

***

Anne and Kris made their way to another wing of the VA for Kris to change her ID card. Wearing a navy skirt and a tasteful ivory and navy sleeveless blouse and carrying an ivory leather handbag, Kris picked her way carefully in navy heels down the VA hallways—looking like a tall fashion model. Her long legs flashed under her navy skirt and from time to time they caught people's eyes, but for the most part no one noticed.

Everywhere Kris stopped to check about her VA business, the desk clerks were pleasant. They seemed to understand that Kris was in a man's body transitioning into a female identity and no one seemed to care.

The Inner SEAL Never Disappears

Kris continued to find support among military friends.

"So how do I look?" Kris asked Justin, a SWAT team leader visiting in town who had stopped by for drinks. It was the first time Justin saw Kris as a girl.

"You look fine," Justin answered, smiling genuinely and accepting a cold beer as he did.

"Tell Anne about how I trained the SWAT teams," Kris said, getting the ball rolling.

"Kris knows how to command respect," Justin said. "He commanded everyone's attention and he let them know that he wasn't going to tolerate their horseplay."

"What did he do that impressed you?" Anne asked, curious to learn how Kris worked.

"He took the time with each one of us and corrected us," Justin explained. "And he made really complex things so simple. He taught us to be smoother in shooting. And in the 'clear and search' training he taught us that you don't have to speak—you make your movements overt so the guys know. It's genius to teach that! Inside the building it was all nonverbal communication." A smile crossed his face as he remembered. "All that training and expertise he's got showed, and everyone felt so much better after he trained us—we all felt so inspired. But it's not only that—that training shows in his life."

"And you are okay with Kris making this change?" Anne asked.

"I met Kris as a man," Justin said, "so he will probably always be that in my mind. But even now, I know the person inside has not changed. The exterior shell doesn't matter. And if it makes him happy, I don't care. After what he's done for our country, he can do whatever he wants—he earned it."

Kris, Anne and Justin talked for a while, then Amie and Walt, Amie's friend from Canada, and Pete joined in the conversation.

"You know as a guy, your whole life you are taught to make fun of transgenders and gays," Justin reflected as the night wore on. "In my job

I see a lot of that. We go to a domestic violence call for a gay couple and someone makes fun, 'Oh it's boyfriend on boyfriend!' Now this with Kris makes me take a step back and think. Life is too short to feel you have to conform to a standard. I know if I was ever out [on the beat] and needed help, I can call Kris. He'd be there in a moment."

"Kris is a good friend," Justin continued quietly. "He is a lot of different things—a great warrior, a great person. This changes how I see gay and transgender people."

Walt, a twenty-something nice young man leaned over to Anne at this point and said in a hushed voice, "I'm in such awe to meet a SEAL. *They make video games and movies about them! I play Black Ops. It's like I met the real person from the games!*"

***

When Kris and Anne returned to Colonel Borjes's house for more photographs, Christy served Kris and Anne burritos and seated them at the family table with the little ones eating alongside them. *She's not afraid to expose her young ones to Kris as a female,* Anne reflected thinking about how Kris's mother had told him that she didn't want him to appear as a female in front of the grandchildren—because it might "infect" them as his first wife Shelly had also feared for Kris's sons.

Going back into the kitchen Karl opened a second bottle and said as he stood at the kitchen counter, "You know I have to be honest with you—this isn't easy for me."

"What's the hard part for you?" Anne asked.

"Well I know you as a guy," Karl answered, smiling with love and respect filling his face as he looked at Kris. "It's just different. I'll get used to it. But it will take some time."

"Kris just had a tough call from her mother," Anne prompted thinking maybe it was best to go easy on Kris for the time being. Karl understood immediately and put his own feelings aside.

"I've seen members of my own family struggle with this too," Christy gently responded, adding. "These things take time."

"It's really a personal thing," Karl commented. "It's your choice how you want to handle it—if you want to come out and live as a woman then that's what you need to do. It's not hurting anyone—except maybe your own kids? Have you told your children?" Karl asked.

"Yes," Kris answered. "I sent a note to Shelly and gave her a heads up in case it comes out in the press. I told her 'I love you as their mother and I love the kids'," Kris explained a look of infinite sadness crossing her face.

"Tell Anne about the training I gave you before you went off to Afghanistan," Kris prompted Karl changing the subject to something less painful.

"Kris probably saved my life!" Karl answered with a big smile crossing his face. "Kris took the time to get me ready for combat," Karl enthusiastically answered. "I remember you pushed me like a drill sergeant. And we almost shot up the Admiral's truck!

It was unreal!" Karl's eyes shined at the memory of it. "It was making me so stressed! You know in our Army training we all stand in a line at the range and the commander yells 'Shoot' and we shoot and then we see how many of us hit the targets. His training was not like that at all! Kris put the Admiral's truck out on the shooting range and he was moving between the targets while I was shooting *live ammunition*!"

Kris and Karl both laughed. "And I'll never forget," Karl continued, "how humble he was afterward. Kris got down and was picking up our shells—cleaning up afterwards. The guys at the range told me later they never saw anybody that senior do that before. They were so impressed."

As they continued Karl reminisced about how Kris had innovated and improved a technology known as the "Crows" in order to foil insurgent attacks.

"We were getting hammered everyday by mortars," Karl explained speaking of Afghanistan. "They liked to hit our trucks. So Kris figured out how to remote the weapon station on top of our trucks, one that we could operate from two hundred meters back."

"With a cable or fiber optic lines," Kris interjected. "The company is doing it as normal gear now when we buy the system."

"So the next time they came to mortar our fire-base," Karl explained with a huge grin on his face, "they thought no one was in the truck—and no one was—but using Kris's system we blasted them!"

Watching them talk, Anne reflected, *Male or female, Kris is still the same person—all the same SEAL skills and experiences as a battle-hardened warrior remain. Despite our culture attributing it to masculinity, it isn't really about male or female—it's about mindset, bravery, loyalty, training and never giving up. Kris is perhaps now facing one of the hardest battles of her life—grasping for and trying to be authentic to herself in both her mind and body. With friends like this she should make it through,* Anne concluded.

CHANGING BODIES—A DREAM FINALLY REALIZED

In a few weeks time, Kris met her doctor at the VA and was started on hormones. The doctor provided one pill to block testosterone and an estrogen patch to slowly deliver female hormones into Kris's body. Kris noticed little effect emotionally—thankfully no hormone swings of puberty, but the physical changes began taking immediate although slow effect. Her skin gradually became softer, although it was already smooth following the laser treatments, and slowly her breasts started to fill in.

"You need to take the hormones for a full year before we'll do surgery," the VA doctor explained. "We want you to be absolutely sure about this transformation—not to have regrets."

"There's nothing I want more," Kris replied, but she understood their reticence to act quickly. Later she would tell Anne, "I've been researching it. Thailand does the most surgeries—they are the experts at it. And they do them at an average age of twenty years old, whereas here most transgenders live under such fear and condemnation that they don't even ask for help until they are around fifty years old on average. That makes a huge difference in their lives."

"I was reading that here in the U.S. when an adolescent raises this issue the medical doctors offer to block puberty so they can take time, go to therapy and figure out what they want to do," Anne shared. "That way, if they decide to change their bodies they don't have to remove unwanted breasts or haven't developed male characteristics that are later hard to change."

"Imagine if I had been offered that?" Kris asked wistfully.

"There are also some cases in the news these days of very young children in kindergarten and first grade claiming they are transgender children," Anne continued. "I find those more troubling because it can also be the parents—if they have their own issues from being sexually assaulted or other issues especially in regard to having a son—who may be projecting their issues onto the child, making the child uncomfortable in his or her own body."

"Yeah, that's a concern," Kris offered, "but little kids also do sense themselves as a gender very early on. I knew before I was in kindergarten. Society just has to catch up."

"It happens for most by four years old. But this is also a complex issue—when it comes to very small children there should probably be some kind of external investigation committee that meets to look carefully into the case, because if it's the parents driving it that's very sad and even abusive," Anne replied. "This latest case involved a child in a boy's body that was going to elementary school as a girl and using the girl's bathroom. The school decided they weren't comfortable with that and wrote a letter to the parents insisting that as long as the child was in a boy's body the child had to use the boy's restroom. It looks like the parents will take a lawsuit over it."

"That kid will get so beat up," Kris answered, clearly identifying with the painfulness of the child's situation. "It would have been so easy for the school to designate a handicap toilet—a single bathroom with a lock on the door as a dual use restroom for cases like that. Why can't they come up with simple but compassionate solutions? It would have been so easy for them—even if they had to construct another bathroom."

Indeed transgender people face so many problems in sorting out their lives. It's hard enough to decide how to come to terms with a body that doesn't match one's gender identity. Should the person struggle to overcome the identification made in childhood? And if so how?

There are no known therapies that guarantee success for such a struggle and many discredited and abusive therapies that simply heap guilt and condemnation upon the person. Some religious leaders are quick to condemn and point these people to more prayer—somehow expecting God to help them suppress the identity they formed as children or come to some supernatural healing, yet religious people can't explain why their God seems to heal some from cancers, broken bones, and other physical ailments and fails to heal others. And there are many histories of transgender persons who tried to find healing in their religions but just found themselves suppressing their gender identity.

Some religions might say to live asexually as the answer—to live without expressing oneself sexually and to forgo a loving sexual connection in life. That too is a tough answer to offer someone who, like all of us, wants to live in love and acceptance and feel connected to others. Usually these religious communities offer a loving community only to those transgender individuals who manage to suppress their longing for a body and a relationship that matches their gender identity. Not many individuals can suppress their sexuality and most people want to live in relationship, perhaps even making a family. Where and how should they find their answers?

A PSYCHOLOGICAL PERSPECTIVE

"Men used to wear heels," Kris commented while he and Anne talked over issues of gender identity. "What is considered male and female is cultural and socially defined. Men used to wear finery, hose, and lace. Now men dress all plain!"

"It's true!" Anne agreed, thinking back to how men in the Victorian ages dressed, like Oscar Wilde, the dandies and their contemporaries wearing fancy buckled shoes with elevated heels.

"And women in Saudi are supposed to cover themselves from head to toe, not drive and be subservient to their men," Kris added. "That wouldn't go over so well here."

Indeed what are considered appropriate gender roles and expression, including dress, for males and females vary considerably as one travels from society to society. It would probably surprise many people to learn that what is considered biologically male and female also has some variance and that there is not complete agreement about what *is* male or female even among medical professionals. For instance, a typical female's sex chromosomes are XX and a typical male's are XY, though some individuals possess XXY, XYY, and XO chromosomes.

Klinefelter syndrome, the non-inherited condition of possessing forty-seven versus forty-six chromosomes and the XXY combination, occurs approximately in one to two out of every thousand births due to a random error in cell division following conception. These children are born with male genitals but are often low on testosterone, may be less muscular than other boys, have less facial and body hair and be infertile.[10]

Turner's syndrome individuals, by contrast, are females who are missing all or part of the second X chromosome in most or all of their cells (designated as XO). Their ovaries do not work properly; they are usually infertile and have a range of other developmental issues. If estrogen replacement therapy is started around age twelve it may trigger the growth of breasts, pubic hair and other sexual characteristics. Turner Syndrome is approximated to occur in one out of two thousand live births.

And intersex is a group of conditions where there is a discrepancy between external and internal genitals. These individuals were up until very recently—in modern Western societies—treated by surgically removing the contradictory organs and reconstructing the external genitalia corresponding to the sex of rearing, a choice often made by physicians or the parents at a very young age with hopes that the gender identity that is later socially constructed (at least in part) will match the body that has been surgically altered. These cases are now often being delayed in surgical resolution until the child has gender identified and can be involved in the choices made.

To many people who have never had the occasion to think deeply about it, there are only two discrete, non-overlapping and completely exclusive categories of sexuality, gender and sexual roles: male and female. And many believe these are predetermined, one or the other, bimodal, black or white—even God ordained—and always aligned in congruence with one's external genitals. But what one believes and perhaps learned growing up is not always correct.

If we look to science for answers, we find some very interesting data. For one thing, human sexuality is not as simple or bimodal as we think. Even the concept of gender is relatively new in our culture. It was only in 1955 that John Money, Ph.D. first used the term "gender" to discuss sexual roles, adding in 1966 the term "gender identity" while conducting his research at Johns Hopkins University. In 1974, Dr. N.W. Fisk coined the term of Gender Dysphoria to signify the mismatch of body and gender.

So where exactly do we get our gender identity and how is it formed? To those of us whose gender identity matches our bodies, it feels inborn. We don't recall all the social and familial forces that shaped us from birth and on into early childhood before we even had formed narrative memory. Gender identity once formed seems always to have been there. But in reality from the moment parents hear "It's a boy," or "It's a girl," they often respond by providing what our culture dictates as gender appropriate responses, which in turn become powerful social forces molding the gender identity that emerges.

There are hundreds of very good scientific gender studies showing how gender can be understood as a socially-constructed identity that relies at least in part on early childhood experience and cultural dictations for the way it unfolds in a person's life. For instance, research shows that the clothes we dress our children in as well as the toys we give them to play with—many of these choices determined only by the external genitalia our children appear with—makes a significant difference in how that child will be responded to and ultimately to that child's sense of self.

In our culture, if one wishes to dress their newborn in gender-neutral clothing they will find it very difficult to do so. And even though we now live in a far more open society where gender divisions of labor are not as strict as they were in the past, there continues to be a giant gender divide in most stores—with the boy "action" toys mostly in blue, gold and black lined up on one aisle, and the pink, fluffy dolls and housekeeping and make-up toys lining the next. The same is true for clothing from birth on—female clothes are often made of pastel colors and soft fabrics featuring depictions of ballerinas, fairies and other fantasy characters, and "boy's" sections will yield blue and brown choices appearing in sturdier fabrics ornamented with trucks, firemen and other "male" icons. Likewise boys are often referred to as "buddy", "tiger", "tough guy", "sport," and girls get called "princess" or "beautiful". And these things all come together to shape a gender identity—one that usually, but not always matches the external genitalia.

Infant researchers have found that the color a baby is dressed in influences how gently the baby is held, how high it's bounced in the air, what vocal tones it is spoken to, etc. and what nicknames it receives, all things that in turn influence how the child views him or herself. So much of what a child responds to in building his or her own sense of self and gender identity is thus socially and culturally derived.

Most children around ages three to five begin to understand the concepts of male and female and identify into one or the other categories by that age. They may even be quite strident about it as they try to figure things out.[11] Children are always intuiting the "rules" they live amongst—the rules of the language, society and culture in which they grow up. And they respond to influences inside the family as well as beyond it, as the culture enters into the home via television, the Internet and as their world expands outside the home in schools, shopping malls, playgrounds, etc.

And these are only the social forces. And while we do know that culture and early experience are highly influential in shaping one's gender identity, we do *not* know if that's the total story. At this point in time, no one really can say how much of gender identity is socially constructed and what may also be driven by genes and environment.

Research showing the effect of hormones and other exposures of the fetus while in utero having an effect in turning certain genes on and also off in subsequent generations is beginning to open up a whole new field of study called epigenetics. This is a field where the interplay of experience and genes is studied, and more and more scientists are beginning to understand that our genetic code does not simply express itself linearly, but instead many of our genes are experience dependent and experience expectant, meaning they rely on our experiences to turn them on or off.

Nowadays there are so many hormone disrupters occurring in our environments—in our food, water and even in the furniture we lay our babies upon, and we have no idea what interaction they also may create between genes, environment and familial-social-cultural forces. Who can say at this stage in our scientific inquiry what the experiences, multi-factorial influences and genes exactly are that may drive human sexuality and gender identity more in one direction than another early on in life?

Transgenderism is no small issue. In the U.S. alone, 700,000 persons identity themselves as transgender individuals. With many uncomfortable to reveal themselves, the true numbers are likely to be far more. Yet if all of these persons are leading lives where they feel trapped inside the wrong body, what are they to do?

Until very recently, the American Psychiatric Association (APA) classified transgender and gender-nonconforming identities as mental disorders. But then in 2013 the APA removed their previous categorization of "Gender Identity Disorder", revising the diagnostic category to "Gender Dysphoria" to reflect the emotional distress that can result from a marked incongruence between one's experienced/expressed gender and assigned gender. This is in recognition that a person's identity is not disordered, but that some transgender people have severe symptoms of gender dysphoria that can be treated successfully.

George Brown, M.D., Professor and Associate Chairman of Psychiatry at East Tennessee State University—previously a military psychiatrist treating transgender service members and veterans for over twenty-five years contemporaneously with many of the events in this book—as well as a ground-breaking researcher concerned with the issues of transgender persons serving in the military has published most of the research studies on transgender phenomena in military and veteran populations and understands these issues better than perhaps anyone else in the world. Brown proposed the theory of flight into hypermasculinity as an explanation for why young transgender male to female (MtF) persons join the military, and why they prefer the more dangerous occupations once enlisted. Indeed his theories likely explain the career path chosen by Chris.

Kris certainly knows there is a great deal of emotional pain in deciding how best to overcome an incongruity between one's gender identity and body, but it might not need to be so awful. How much of the mental anguish is a result of social or religious condemnation and bullying that doesn't need to be there?

Some Christians believe that a growing and vibrant Christian life is incompatible with being identified as a transgender individual. But it's so easy to condemn others, particularly when their struggles are so different and alien from one's own. If being transgender is a "sin", then where does the blame go? To God who willed it? To the social forces and beyond who helped to construct the gender identity? To the person himself or herself?

There are so many sexual acts that really do harm others: sexual molestation, sexual assaults, rapes, violent actions that rob innocents of their entire lives, infidelities and the lies that go with them which often break families apart and devastate innocent children, irresponsible conceptions resulting in unwanted and unloved children, or abortions that if done later in pregnancy may cause a human fetal child suffering. These things occur in the millions each day. Can a transgender individual find love and acceptance alongside those who also practice these acts?

Perhaps before condemning someone struggling with these very painful issues as Kris has, these persons should consider that if there is such a thing as a soul—an eternal being that transcends our body when we die—it's not likely to have a gender. The soul—if it exists—is an energetic being full of light and love.

The most important question might be: What can we do to feed the soul of these persons? To find answers to their struggle for love and acceptance?

This is Kris's story and it's not over yet. From early childhood, Chris Beck was aching to his inner core over his feelings of mismatch between his body and his gender identity—the socially-constructed and perhaps genetically- and environmentally-derived sense of self that was formed in childhood and persisted to this day.

Kris was, from early childhood onward, a female that did not match the male body she was caught inside. Kris could try in therapy to address the traumas that occurred in her childhood—hard work requiring a lot of money and time and sadness. But we know that many abuse victims grow up with none of these gender identity issues, and transgender individuals also come from perfectly loving families. So would it do any good? In terms of helping Kris to come to peace with the angst she felt as a child and the safe places she found in response to hardships endured then—and later, both in war and in transition, yes. In terms of changing her gender identity, highly unlikely.

Kris has chosen to change her body to match her mind by undergoing hormone treatment and surgery, a choice that holds the guarantee of gaining congruency and the possibility to live an authentic life. While surgically changing one's body is radical, it is not so different from people who get nose jobs, breast implants or the other thousands of alterations done to increase self esteem and create more peace with one's external appearance.

There is also a middle ground that many take: facing and coming to terms with the feeling of disconnect between the gender identity and the body. Although when it comes to expressing one's sexuality as a female in a male's body or vice versa, things do become complicated—just as they are once one has transitioned to a new body. The solution then mainly depends on finding a loving and accepting partner willing to work with things as they are.

One thing is for sure—there are no simple or easy answers.

For Kris, moving forward as a female means claiming her third life—as a Warrior Princess. In her mind, the first life is what she was born into, a life she had no choices about. The second life is what she moved into based upon the first, often making poor choices or following decisions made early in life. But her third life is all about taking personal responsibility, forming and following her values and having valor—making the choices she believes are the right ones and having the courage to step into them.

Transgender is a tough problem, but Kris is a tough girl and she knows she's going to win this one, just like she made it through the BUD/S training to join the SEALs. She is going to find the way to live fully and authentically—having found a congruence between mind, soul and body.

And it is her hope that as others make their journeys, searching in their own hearts and minds for their paths to healing from whatever pain and suffering that life has dealt to them, that they will always remember that love is the greatest guiding force in this life.

ACKNOWLEDGMENTS

A special thanks for reviewing and commenting on the book to: Tiffany Ashcom; Lieutenant Colonel Karl Borjes; George Brown, M.D.; Andrew Citino; Dave Davanay, CWO4 (ret.); Michael Everett, SOC (ret.); Randi Ettner, Ph.D.; Kathleen Farrell, Ph.D.; Jamison Green, Ph.D.; Travis Lively; Indra Lusero, J.D.; Commander William (Shep) Shepherd and Professor Kevan Wylie, MD and the SOCOM Public Affairs Office. and the SOCOM Public Affairs Office. Thank you especially to George Brown, M.D., who also provided helpful advice regarding many definitional and treatment issues, and to Indra Lusero, who commented helpfully on transgender treatment issues. Thanks to Shep for his friendship and support to Kris and for his heartfelt and ever so kindly-written foreword. Anne also thanks Commander Todd Veazie for inviting her into work on the SEALs resilience project and all that it led to—thanks for the ride, Todd! Thanks also to our fantastic editor Jayne Pillemer for her thoughtful insights, great job editing, support and her most valuable advice throughout the process. Thanks to Nikki Hensley for the super layout and book design of all of the various digital and print versions of this book. Thanks to artist Jessica Speckhard for creatively contributing to the front cover artwork. And thanks to all those who fight for the health, safety and rights of the LGBT community and especially to the Trevor project for being there for those in dire need.

ABOUT THE AUTHORS

Kristin Beck, born Christopher Beck, was born in 1966 in New York. He grew up on a farm in the hills of western Pennsylvania. Graduated from Wellsville High school in 1984, he went on to Virginia Military Institute majoring in Electrical Engineering. He then graduated from Alfred University in 1989 with a BA in Political Science.

After the U.S. responded to Iraq's invasion of Kuwait in 1990, he enlisted in the Navy and went directly to SEAL Training, Basic Underwater Demolition (BUD/S Class 179). He graduated the top of his class.

His initial SEAL tour was with SEAL Team One from 1992-1999 where he completed 7 SEAL Platoon deployments, including two combat tours. He was recognized with one Army and four Navy Achievement Medals for his operational innovations and his tactical prowess as a Special Operator.

Chris was then selected to join the SEAL two-star headquarters, Naval Special Warfare Command (WARCOM), to assist in the development of an automated mission planning system (SWAMPS). This effort was at a standstill as a result of poor contractor performance; Chief Beck created completely new system architecture and wrote its source code in his spare time. This program has been the basis for SOF mission planning to this day and is now a $60M program, still used every day by hundreds of SOF operators.

Chief Beck was deployed to the Pacific and Indian Ocean with SEAL Team Five in 2002 in support of the Global War on Terror. During this deployment, using his skills as a Navy Quartermaster, he developed a novel method for precise small boat navigation, which enabled long-range VBSS (Visit Board Search and Seizure) missions. He combined WWII maneuvering board techniques, GPS, and vectoring from P3 aircraft, to create new tactical capabilities. SEALs now routinely drop rubber boats in mid-ocean for long range intercepts using SCPO Beck's techniques.

He deployed again in 2003 to Kuwait and conducted special operations with small UAVs in the opening phase of Operation "Iraqi Freedom". Chief Beck was awarded the Navy Commendation Medal with Combat "V" for his efforts with American and British forces in Basrah, Iraq.

In 2005, Senior Chief Beck was board selected to transfer to Naval Special Warfare Development Group (DEVGRU) to head the UAV Department and Special Reconnaissance units. He was the primary Subject Matter Expert in the Pathfinder UAV technology demonstration and ewas instrumental in development of the Small and Medium class UAVs in use by Special Operations Forces to this day.

He was then selected to be the Tactical Surveillance Department head, leading the entire overseas surveillance and field R&D effort for his Special Operations Component Command. He directed $16M of procurement and over $300M in R&D efforts in this period. Senior Chief Beck also worked with key senior leaders and executives from OSD, DDR&E and SOCOM on the Hostile Forces Tagging Tracking and Locating (HFTTL) "Quick Look" assessment. His operational inputs and technical expertise became the foundation for OSD's TTL development strategy. Over the next five years the HFTTL initiative became a $600M OSD program. SCPO Beck received the Defense Meritorious Service Medal for his accomplishments during this period.

In 2008, Senior Chief Beck received a special assignment to the Joint Task Force in Afghanistan and became a primary HUMINT source handler for operations along the eastern Afghan border. He conducted over 200 clandestine source operations and led sniper and ladder teams on numerous high-risk missions—he was the Ground Force Commander and primary entry team leader on a special "High Value Target" capture. He received the Purple Heart and Bronze Star with combat "V" in these operations.

In 2009, Senior Chief Beck was requested to become the Senior Enlisted Advisor to USSOCOM's Science Advisor and the S&T Directorate. He has been intimately engaged in all of the key technologies and advanced development efforts at the command. His efforts are critical to providing cutting edge technologies to SOF personnel in support of Special Operations Forces Worldwide.

While at SOCOM Senior Chief Beck developed and led the rapid innovation and prototyping shops now called the Mobile Technology and Repair Complex (MTRC). The MTRC deployed to Afghanistan, and is now forward creating tactical advantages and new mission capabilities daily for SOF units. It is now a Program of Record and an enduring requirement for all contingency operations.

In 2010, Senior Chief Beck was named in Congressional testimony by the Honorable Zachary Lemnios, Director Defense Research and Engineering in connection to the MTRC and his many SOF innovations.

On assignment to assist OSD experts, SCPO Beck co-authored a far-reaching study on the hydrology of the Helmand Province. He then personally developed a technical solution to counter the dwindling water tables in the area, which was to be adopted by USAID.

As a result of his outstanding achievements, technical innovations and positive impacts in the SOF community, SCPO Beck received the coveted NDIA 2010 Special Operations/ Low Intensity Conflict Achievement Award.

Since leaving Active Duty in 2011, Chris Beck has been working as a Senior Consultant for LMI, Logistics Management Institute, and has become a lead on many projects and is constantly consulted in projects ranging from Counter Threat Finance to Logistic displacement of vehicles currently in Afghanistan. He has co-authored and advised on various projects for the Departments.

He was selected to duty in the Office of the Secretary of Defense in the Rapid Reaction Technology Office (RRTO) in April 2012. He has since developed many technologies that will be in the warfighters hands soon.

Chris announced his intentions to live his life as a woman in the beginning of 2013. Now, Kristin intends to be an activist in an effort to bring understanding and compassion for the Transgender community and wishes to continue her service to Peace and Freedom.

Anne Speckhard, Ph.D. is Adjunct Associate Professor of Psychiatry at Georgetown University Medical School. Dr. Speckhard has been working in the field of posttraumatic stress disorder (PTSD) since the 1980s and has extensive experience working in Europe, the Middle East and the former Soviet Union. She has provided expert consultation to European and Middle Eastern governments as well as the U.S. Department of Defense, NATO, OSCE and other organization regarding programs for prevention and rehabilitation of individuals committed to political violence and militant jihad. In 2006-2007, she worked with the U.S. Department of Defense to design and pilot test the Detainee Rehabilitation Program in Iraq. In 2002, she interviewed hostages taken in the Moscow Theater about their psychological responses and observations of the suicidal terrorists and did the same in 2005 with surviving hostages from the Beslan school take-over. Since 2002, she has collected more than four hundred research interviews of family members, friends, close associates and hostages of terrorists and militant jihadi extremists in various parts of the world. Dr. Speckhard is also the director of the Holocaust Survivors Oral Histories Project – Belarus, a project constructing the history of the Minsk Ghetto and Holocaust in Belarus through oral histories and archival research. Dr. Speckhard consults to governments and lectures to security experts worldwide. She is the author of *Talking to Terrorists: Understanding the Psycho-Social Motivations of Militant Jihadi Terrorists, Mass Hostage Takers, Suicide Bombers and "Martyrs"* and *Fetal Abduction: The True Story of Multiple Personalities and Murder.*

Website: www.AnneSpeckhard.com

GLOSSARY

AK 47 – an assault rifle first developed in the former USSR, also known as a Kalashnikov.

Agent Orange – the code name for Herbicide Orange (HO) and Agent LNC, one of the herbicides and defoliants used by the U.S. Department of Defense during the Vietnam War from 1961-1971. It was later blamed for numerous health problems of those exposed to it.

Asexual – a lack of sexual interest or attraction to anyone, can also be a lack of sexual orientation.

Basrah – a city in southern Iraq.

Blood chit – an official notice carried by members of the military, requesting assistance in local languages of civilians in enemy territory.

BUD/S – Basic Underwater Demolition/SEAL training consisting of a six-month SEAL training course held at the Naval Special Warfare Training Center in Coronado, CA. It begins with a five-week instruction and pre-training followed by three phases of grueling BUD/S training in which many participants drop or are failed out.

Care Coalition – the advocacy support unit for the health and readiness of the United States Special Operations Command (SOCOM) also providing support to wounded, ill or injured warriors and their families.

Chinook – the Boeing CH-47 "Chinook" heavy-lift helicopter used for troop movement, artillery emplacement and battlefield resupply.

(Security) Clearance – a status granted by the U.S. government to certain individuals to allow them access to classified information following a thorough background check.

Crossdressing (transvestism)* - Wearing clothing and adopting a gender role presentation that, in a given culture, is more typical of the other sex.

Cymbalta – an antidepressant made of duloxetine, a selective serotonin and norepinephrine reuptake inhibitor.

DShK – a Soviet heavy machine gun.

DOD – United States Department of Defense.

Dalai Lama – the spiritual leader of Tibetan Buddhism considered by his followers to be reborn as a bodhisattva of compassion.

(Operation) Desert Storm – a military operation in the United States-led Gulf War, waged August 2, 1990 to February 28, 1991 by a U.N.-authorized Coalition force of thirty-four nations against Iraq in response to Iraq's invasion and annexation of Kuwait.

Don't Ask/Don't Tell – the official United States policy from December 21, 1993 to September 20, 2011, which prohibited military personnel from discriminating against or harassing hidden gay, lesbian and bisexuals serving in the military while barring openly gay, lesbian or bisexual persons from military service. It did not address transgender individuals who were at the time and are still barred by Department of Defense regulations from serving in the military, according to their view of transgender as a medically disqualifying condition.

Extortion 17 – the call sign of the Chinook military helicopter, which was shot down while transporting a quick reaction force in Afghanistan. The crash killed all thirty-eight aboard including seventeen SEALS, three NSW support personnel, three AFSOC operators, one Combat Controller and two Pararescuemen, all members of the 24th Special Tactics Squadron. Their deaths are the greatest single loss of life ever suffered by the U.S. Special Operations community in the 24-year history of the U.S. Special Operations Command.

Falwell, Reverend Jerry – an American evangelical fundamentalist Southern Baptist preacher and political conservative who founded the Moral Majority in 1979.

Fast-rope/fast-roping – also known as fast rope insertion extraction system (FRIES); a technique for descending from a helicopter by holding onto a thick rope with gloved hands and sliding down it.

Forward operating base/FOB – a secured forward military position, sometimes including an airfield, hospital or other facitilies used to support tactical operations.

Frogman – someone trained in scuba diving or underwater swimming in a tactical capacity including combat.

GAF – Ground Assault Force.

Gasparilla – Gasparilla Pirate Festival is an annual celebration held each year in late January or early February in Tampa, Florida celebrating the apocryphal legend of Jose Gaspar, a mythical Spanish pirate captain who is said to have operated in Southwest Florida.

Gender Dysphoria* – Distress that is caused by a discrepancy between a person's gender identity and that person's sex assigned at birth (and the associated gender role and/or primary and secondary sex characteristics) (Fisk, 1974; Knudson, De Cuypere, & Bockting, 2010).

Gender Identity* – A person's intrinsic sense of being male (a boy or a man), female (a girl or woman), or an alternative gender (e.g., boygirl, girl-boy, transgender, genderqueer, eunuch) (Bockting, 1999; Stoller, 1964).

Gender Identity Disorder* – Formal diagnosis set forth by the Diagnostic Statistical Manual of Mental Disorders, 4th Edition, Text Rev (DSM IV-TR) (American Psychiatric Association, 2000). Gender identity disorder is characterized by a strong and persistent cross-gender identification and a persistent discomfort with one's sex or sense of inappropriateness in the gender role of that sex, causing clinically significant distress or impairment in social, occupational, or other important areas of functioning. (Author's note - This diagnosis was removed and replaced with Gender Dysphoria by the American Psychiatric Association in May 2013).

Gender nonconforming* - Adjective to describe individuals whose gender identity, role, or expression differs from what is normative for their assigned sex in a given culture and historical period.

Gender role or expression* - Characteristics in personality, appearance, and behavior that in a given culture and historical period are designated as masculine or feminine (that is, more typical of the male or female social role) (Ruble, Martin, & Berenbaum, 2006). While most individuals present socially in clearly male or female gender roles, some people present in an alternative gender role such as genderqueer or specifically transgender. All people tend to incorporate both masculine and feminine characteristics in their gender expression in varying ways and to varying degrees (Bockting, 2008).

Genderqueer* - Identity label that may be used by individuals whose gender identity and/or role does not conform to a binary understanding of gender as limited to the categories of man or woman, male or female (Bockting, 2008).

GMV – Ground Mobility Vehicle is a special operations version of the Humvee.

HAF – Helicopter Assault Force.

Honor Man – the most outstanding man of the Basic Underwater Demolition/SEAL (BUD/S) class, "whose sheer force of example inspires his classmates to keep going when they're ready to quit".

Hooyah – the battle cry used by the Navy SEALs, often used to say "okay" or "understood" or to show enthusiasm.

IED – improvised explosive device.

Intel – military intelligence or information in general.

Inter-sex/inter-sexed – a genital ambiguity caused by a combination of chromosomal genotype and sexual phenotype other than XY-male and XX female that do not allow an individual to be distinctly identified as male or female.

Irregular warfare – warfare in which one or more of the combatants are non-state actors and are not part of regular forces as recognized by the Geneva Convention.

Kyle, Chris – a well-known Navy SEAL sniper who after his service started a charity to support veterans with PTSD. Kyle was tragically killed when a veteran he was trying to help cope with his posttraumatic stress disorder turned his gun upon Kyle and shot him dead.

LGBT – the lesbian, gay, bisexual and transgender community.

LAW rocket – light anti-tank weapon, specifically a portable one-shot 66 mm unguided anti-tank weapon.

Leydig cells – cells in the testicle that produce testosterone and other androgen hormones in the presence of luteinizing hormone.

Little Bird – the light helicopters used U.S. special operations forces

MH-53 – a series of long-range combat search and rescue helicopters used by the U.S. Air Force to vertically insert special operations troops into battle.

Male-to-Female (MtF)* - Adjective to describe individuals assigned male at birth who are changing or who have changed their body and/or gender role from birth-assigned male to a more feminine body or role.

Mortar – an indirect fire weapon that shoots explosive projectiles called mortar bombs at low velocities, short range and in high-arching paths.

Muezzin – the person at a mosque appointed to lead and recite the call to prayer usually using a melodious chanting voice.

Mujahideen – Arabic word literally referring to those who struggle or people doing jihad. In militant groups it refers to a "holy warrior".

NATO Stabilization Force/SFOR – a NATO-led multi-national peace-keeping force deployed to Bosnia and Herzegovina following the Bosnian war to deter hostilities, stabilize the peace and contribute to a secure environment with the goal of a lasting consolidation of peace.

OGA – other government agencies.

OSD – Office of the Secretary of Defense, United States Department of Defense.

Pashto – the native language of the Pashtun people of South-Central Asia.

Posttraumatic stress disorder/PTSD – a severe and debilitating anxiety disorder triggered by the experience of a terrifying event. PTSD symptoms include re-experiencing the traumatic event in flashbacks, nightmares, hallucinations, etc.; avoidance of stimuli associated with the trauma; increased bodily arousal including difficulty falling or staying asleep, inability to concentrate, irritability or bouts of anger and hypervigilance. PTSD symptoms last longer than one month and cause significant impairment in social, occupational, or other important areas of functioning.

Ranger/United States Army Rangers – the elite infantry of the United States Army.

Raven – a small, unmanned aircraft system (drone) that provides real-time direct situational awareness and target information.

Republican Guards – the elite troops of the Iraqi army reporting directly to Saddam Hussein.

RuPaul – an American actor, drag queen, model, author and recording artist.

S&T – Science & Technology.

SEAL – United States Navy Sea, Air, Land Teams, commonly known as the Navy SEALs, are the U.S. Navy's principal special operations force and a part of the Naval Special Warfare Command and the United States Special Operations Command.

Sex* - Sex is assigned at birth as male or female, usually based on the appearance of the external genitalia. When the external genitalia are ambiguous, other components of sex (internal genitalia, chromosomal and hormonal sex) are considered in order to assign sex (Grumbach, Hughes, & Conte, 2003; MacLaughlin & Donahoe, 2004; Money & Ehrhardt, 1972; Vilain, 2000). For most people, gender identity and expression are consistent with their sex assigned at birth; for transsexual, transgender, and gender nonconforming individuals, gender identity or expression differ from their sex assigned at birth.

Sex reassignment surgery (gender affirmation surgery)* - Surgery to change primary and/or secondary sex characteristics to affirm a person's gender identity. Sex reassignment surgery can be an important part of medically necessary treatment to alleviate gender dysphoria.

Shura – Arabic word meaning consultation and refers to the practice of collective decision making by Muslims in organizing their affairs.

SWAT – Special Weapons and Tactics; a name used for law enforcement units that use military-style light weapons and specialized tactics in high-risk operations that fall outside of the capabilities of regular uniformed police.

Six plate – custom shooting targets made of six "plates" set up on a rack.

Special Operations – unconventional military operations performed independently or in conjunction with conventional military operations.

Special Air Service/SAS – a special forces regiment of the British Army.

SOCOM – United States Special Operations Command.

SWCC – the U.S. Navy's Special Warfare Combatant-craft Crewmen; the special operations force who operate and maintain the small craft used to support special operations missions of the U.S. Navy SEALs.

T-girl – a male to female transgender with a female gender identity.

Taliban – an Islamic fundamentalist political movement in Afghanistan made up mainly of Pashtun tribesmen that took power, ruling as the Islamic Emirate of Afghanistan from September 1996 to December 2001 with Kandahar as its capital. The Taliban enforced a very strict interpretation of Sharia law including brutal repression of women. After 9-11 the Taliban were overthrown by the U.S. led invasion of Afghanistan, but they regrouped as an insurgent movement to fight the U.S.-backed Karzai government and the NATO-led International Security Assistance Force (ISAF).

Thobe – an ankle length garment, usually with long sleeves, worn by men in Arabic parts of the world.

Tradecraft – techniques used in modern espionage and intelligence gathering.

Transgender* - Adjective to describe a diverse group of individuals who cross or transcend culturally defined categories of gender. The gender identity of transgender people differs to varying degrees from the sex they were assigned at birth (Bockting, 1999).

Transition* - Period of time when individuals change from the gender role associated with their sex assigned at birth to a different gender role. For many people, this involves learning how to live socially in "the other" gender role; for others this means finding a gender role and expression that is most comfortable for them. Transition may or may not include feminization or masculinization of the body through hormones or other medical procedures. The nature and duration of transition is variable and individualized.

Transsexual* - Adjective (often applied by the medical profession) to describe individuals who seek to change or who have changed their primary and/or secondary sex characteristics through femininizing or masculinizing medical interventions (hormones and/or surgery), typically accompanied by a permanent change in gender role. (Author's note: George Brown M.D. offered this further explanation - Transsexual/transsexuality* – the condition in which a person either identifies with a gender not associated with their assigned sex and desires to live and be accepted as a member of the opposite sex or wants to live as a third gender or genderqueer, usually accompanied by a sense of discomfort with, or inappropriateness of one's anatomic sex, and a wish to have surgery and hormonal treatment to make one's body as congruent as possible with one's preferred sex. Transsexuals are the minority of transgender persons and have such severe gender dysphoria that they usually seek medical and surgical treatments to align their bodies with their subjective gender identity. Most untreated transsexuals meet diagnostic criteria in the American Psychiatric Association's Diagnostic and Statistical Manual V (DSM V) for gender dysphoria.

Transgender people by contrast, may or may not have a diagnosis of gender dysphoria and may or may not seek medical procedures. Transgender is more of an umbrella term.).

Traumatic bereavement – grief resulting from the loss of a loved one in a traumatic incident, may be similar to posttraumatic stress disorder.

Trident – the Special Warfare insignia of U.S. Navy SEALs, signifying the individual's completion of the Navy's Basic Underwater Demolition/SEAL (BUD/S) training and SEAL Qualification Training and has been designated as a U.S. Navy SEAL.

UAV – unmanned aerial vehicle, or drone, is an aircraft that operates without a human pilot on board. It is controlled either autonomously by computers in the vehicle or under the remote control of a pilot on the ground or in another vehicle.

Underwater Demolition Teams (UDT) – an elite special forces established by the U.S. Navy during World War II, whose primary function was to reconnoiter and destroy using explosives and enemy defensive obstacles on beaches prior to amphibious landings, as well as to breach cables and nets protecting enemy harbors, plant limpet minds on enemy ships and locate and mark mines for clearing. They were the precursors to the U.S. Navy SEALs.

United States Marines/U.S. Marines/USMC Valor – a branch of the United States Armed Forces responsible for providing power projection from the sea to rapidly deliver combined arms task forces.

Vampire hours – awake at night, sleeping during daylight hours.

Vehicle borne improvised explosive device (VBIED) – an explosive-laden vehicle used as a car or truck bomb.

Vicodin – a medication made of acetaminophen and hydrocodone used to relieve moderate to severe pain. Vicodin is in a group of drugs called opioid pain relievers, is sometimes called a narcotic, and can be habit forming and abused by persons with drug abuse or addiction issues.

War on Terror – also known as the Global War on Terrorism refers to the international military campaign to eliminate al Qaeda and other militant terrorist organizations and the regimes accused of supporting them. The War on Terror was started by U.S. President George Bush in response to the 9-11 attacks on the United States, and the UK and other NATO and non-NATO nations participate in the conflict. President Obama refers to these operations as the Overseas Contingency Operation.

*All starred definitions are taken from the World Professional Association for Transgender Health (WPATH) Standards of Care (see bibliography for reference).

Resources We Found Helpful

Well-Known Transgender People

List of well-known people who are transgender –

http://en.wikipedia.org/wiki/List_of_transgender_people

Helpful Information in Supporting Transgender Individuals

GLAAD's Transgender Resources –

http://www.glaad.org/transgender

Legal Advocacy and Justice Issues

American Civil Liberties Union (ACLU) –

http://www.aclu.org/translaw

Injustice at Every Turn: A Report of the National Transgender Discrimination Survey

http://www.thetaskforce.org/downloads/reports/reports/ntds_full.pdf

Lambda Legal –

http://www.lambdalegal.org/issues/transgender-rights

National Center for Lesbian Rights –

http://www.nclrights.org/site/PageServer?pagename=issue_transgender

National Center for Transgender Equality –

http://transequality.org

Sylvia Rivera Law Project (legal advocacy section) –

http://srlp.org/

Transgender Law Center –

http://transgenderlawcenter.org

Military & Veterans Support Networks for LGBT Community

Outserve Magazine –

http://outservemag.com/tag/transgender-military/

Palm Center – An organization that commissions research in the area of gender, sexuality and the military, found at http://www.palmcenter.org, with their Transgender Military Initiative found at http://www.palmcenter.org/people/indra-lusero

Servicemembers Legal Defense Network-Outserve –

http://www.sldn.org

Transgender American Veterans Association –

http://www.tavausa.org

Veterans Health Administration's (VA) Transgender Policy in the Military –

http://www.va.gov/vhapublications/ViewPublication.asp?pub_ID=2863

Suicide Prevention & Violence Mitigation Resources

National Suicide Prevention Hotline– 1-800-Suicide (784-2433)

National Sexual Assault Hotline– 1-800-656-Hope (4673)

National Domestic Violence Hotline– 1-800-799-Safe (7233)

The Trevor Project is a national organization providing crisis intervention and suicide prevention services to LGBT and questioning youth. The Trevor Lifeline (serving U.S. residents only) can be reached 24/7 at 1-866-488-7386. Their live chat, available in more limited hours, can be accessed via this site:

http://www.thetrevorproject.org/lifelinechat

Transgender Suicide Report by Laura Amato is found at: http://www.lauras-playground.com/transgender_suicide_report.htm. The Online Support Moderated Chat Room for Transgender Individuals who are trained in Youth Suicide Prevention is live at

http://www.lauras-playground.com/chat.htm

Professional Resources

The World Professional Association for Transgender Health. (2013). Standards of Care for the Health of Transsexual, Transgender, and Gender Nonconforming People, 7th Version found at: http://www.wpath.org/documents/Standards%20of%20Care%20V7%20-%202011%20WPATH.pdf

1 "Many firefights last five minutes but they seem like forever," Kris recalls of combat. "Sometimes it's a few hours and it seems like ten minutes. It's all relative to what you are doing at the time and the experience you have, it even depends on who you are fighting next to—who's got your six [back]." Kris also recalls the first free fall jump: "It was from 12,000 feet up. When I jumped it felt like I was in free fall for about five seconds and that it was a night jump—in actuality it was a minute or so and in broad daylight! The next jump seemed to be ten seconds and so on. When you got over the rush and accustomed to it, time returned to normal and then when you got really good, you could slow time down and really concentrate on the fine details. You become an artist."

2 This chapter represents a composite of actual firefights in Afghanistan but for security reasons this is not an exact history.

3 This chapter contains conjecture on Luther's mental workings based upon his comments, his behavior and what we know about his past.

4 Kris adds that the training and development of the SEAL didn't end after this first year of "torture"—there was a whole additional year as a "FNG", learning additional "skills" such as washing spray glue from one's entire body while his legs were taped together, along with many other great "lessons" gleaned from "special training after hours". Only after getting back from that first "deployment" learning advanced skills and working with our foreign counterparts did Chris rise to the level of a "One Platoon Wonder". In the SEALs, the training never ceases.

5 Later John would find his center and master many other skills, becoming a combat-proven asset to the Special Boat Squadrons while Chris would win his way into the SEALs. John and Kris remain good friends to this day.

6 Later John would find his center and master many other skills, becoming a combat-proven asset to the Special Boat Squadrons while Chris would win his way into the SEALs. John and Kris remain good friends to this day.

7 Kris recalls, "In those days there was no drinking on the compound, so ramshackle hooch had been built just outside the fence. It was nicer than the Quonset huts of the original 'Niland', but it wasn't a great place; tearing it down for the fire shouldn't have been a big deal. But this is the military and we paid for that shack and for our 'goofing off' for quite some time—Choate remembers it well."

8 Kristin states, "a REMF is a Rear Echelon Mother F*@#er; a FOBIT is the modern version of REMF. Basically the guys who stay at the HQ and push papers and never go to the field."

9 Todd Veazie and Anne had been working together and Anne had already met with Rear Admiral Sean Pybus of Navy SEALs Special Warfare Group to obtain his blessing on the study and also with Jim Smith of the

Navy SEALs foundation who were supporting it although it was slow going at that time.

10 Up to a third of these boys may develop enlarged breast tissue in pu berty. Some affected individuals may also have genital differences such as undescended testes, a very small penis, or the opening of the urethra on the underside of the penis. With early diagnosis and testosterone re-placement therapy, boys with this syndrome can grow up to have nor-mal sexual lives, increased chances of fertility and develop male physi-cal characteristics such as body hair, musculature, etc., and avoid breast development.

11 Anne recalls her preschool son, Danny, insisting to his older sisters that only boys can ride motorcycles and go to the hardware store and when his sisters argued with him, he conceded that girls can ride on the back of motorcycles—hanging on to the men. Where he got those concepts no one was sure—perhaps television—but nevertheless as a young boy it was important for him to insist up and consolidate his gender iden-tity based on available stereotypes. And recently, Anne's three-year-old granddaughter decided that men wear short hair and belts whereas girls have long hair. When she was put into a dress with a belt she ques-tioned. "Aren't belts for boys?"—and required reassurance that this was a "girl's" belt. At four years old she insists that pink is for girls and that blue is for boys despite being raised in a liberal household that does not impose such stereotypes.

BIBLIOGRAPHY

Association, A. P. (2000). *Diagnostic & Statistic Manual of Mental Disorders (DSM-IV-TR)*. Washington, D.C.: American Psychiatric Association Press.

Association, A. P. (2013). *Diagnostic & Statistic Manual of Mental Disorders (DSM-5(TM))*. Washington, D.C.: American Psychiatric Association Press.

Bockting, W. O. (2008). Psychotherapy and the real-life experience: From gender dichotomy to gender diversity. *Sexologies,* 17(4), 211-224.

Bockting, W. O. (1999). From construction to context: Gender through the eyes of the transgendered. *Siecus Report,* 28(1), 3-7.

Brown, G. R. (1988). Transsexuals in the military: flight into hypermasculinity. *Archives of Sexual Behavior,* 17(6), 527-537.

Brown, G. R. (1989). Current legal status of transsexualism in the military (letter). *Archives of Sexual Behavior,* 18(4), 371-373.

Belkin, A., Whitten, T., Brown, G., & Melms, M. (2008). Gender Identity and the Military (Abstract). *International Journal of Transgenderism,* 10(3), 174.

Fisk, N. M. (1974). Editorial: Gender dysphoria syndrome--the conceptualization that liberalizes indications for total gender reorientation and implies a broadly based multi-dimensional rehabilitative regimen. *Western Journal of Medicine,* 120(5), 386-391.

Grumbach, M. M., Hughes, I. A., & Conte, F. (2003). Disorders of sex differentiation. In P. R. Larsen, H. M. Kronenberg, S. Melmed & K. S. Polonsky (Eds.), *Williams textbook of endocrinology* (10 ed., pp. 842-1002). Philadelphia, PA: Saunders.

Knudson, G., De Cuypere, G., & Bockting, W. (2010). Recommendations for revision of the DSM diagnoses of gender identity disorders: Consensus statement of The World Professional Association for Transgender Health. *International Journal of Transgenderism* 12(2), 115-118.

McDuffie, E., & Brown, G. R. (2010). Veterans with Gender Identity Disturbances: A Descriptive Study. *International Journal of Transgenderism,* 12(1).

MacLaughlin, D. T. (Donahoe, P.K.). Sex determination and differentiation. *New England Journal of Medicine,* 350(4), 367-378.

Money, J., & Ehrhardt, A. A. (1972). *Man and woman, boy and girl.* Baltimore, MD: The Johns Hopkins University Press.

Ruble, D. N., Martin, C. L., & Berenbaum, S. A. (2006). Gender development *Handbook of child psychology* (6th ed., pp. 858-932). Hoboken, NJ: John Wiley & Sons, Inc.

Stoller, R. J. (1964). A contribution to the study of gender identity. *Interna-*

tional Journal of Psychoanalysis, 45, 220-226.

The World Professional Association for Transgender Health. (2013). Standards of Care for the Health of Transsexual, Transgender, and Gender Nonconforming People, 7th Version. Retrieved from http://www. wpath.org/documents/Standards%20of%20Care%20V7%20-%20 2011%20WPATH.pdf

Vilain, E. (2000). Genetics of sexual development. *Annual Review of Sex Research*, 11, 1-25.

Index

CPSIA information can be obtained at www.ICGtesting.com
Printed in the USA
LVOW131611230613

339841LV00002B/5/P